Memoirs

Covering period 1915-1947

Douglas Farmiloe

Memoirs

By

Douglas Farmiloe

Published by Douglas Farmiloe

In conjunction with

The Matching Press, Harlow

Published by

Douglas Farmiloe

Henstead Hall, Henstead

Beccles, Suffolk, NR347LD

Tel 01502 740371, Email: g.d.farmiloe@btconnect.com

In conjunction with

The Matching Press

1 Watermans End, Matching Green, Harlow, Essex, CM170RQ

Tel 01279 731308, Email: sptstreeter@aol.com

Printed in Great Britain by

Spiegl Press Limited

42 Guash Way, Ryhall Road, Stamford, Lincolnshire, PE9 1XH.

Copyright 2010 G.D.Farmiloe

British Library Cataloguing in Publication Data

Farmiloe, Douglas

A Memoir

1. A Tarnished Silver Spoon

ISBN -978-0-9518664-5-0

Myself, aged 21, 1936,

To Jacqui

Introduction

The idea of writing my memoirs first came to light in 1989 when I wrote to my daughter giving a shortened version of my life. Susan went to the USA at the age of eight years for a period, which was supposed to be for just two years. The promise to return my daughter was renegaded on for a number of reasons and I did not see my daughter again for thirty eight years until June 1990.
Despite all this our relationship of father and daughter is very close today.

My son first went to the USA at the age of thirteen but our relationship has been made more fortuitous as Michael has spent his whole life living either side of the Atlantic.

This gap of so many years has meant that I never knew my three grandsons until they were married men. On the other hand I have been a witness to a number of my fifteen great grandchildren reaching adulthood.

It was in 2009 that I seriously started writing these memoirs in earnest. In fact I did not refer to my earlier attempts when writing the present version.

My life has been dominated by spending too much money, booze and my love of the opposite sex. Although I have had many flirtations there were five special relationships of which four will be discussed in these memoirs. The missing relationship refers to a lady I met in 1945 who has sadly passed away as recently as 2010. I have deliberately omitted any reference to her in these memoirs except for one paragraph to save her and her family any possible embarrassment.

Even today my life is dominated by the magic number of 5 women, whom I am constantly in contact with at work: Maxine and Jacqui. My daughter Sheba whom I see almost every day my other daughter Helen and Karen a (great friend).

Although one would get the impression that I am dominated by the female species this is far from true. All my life I have been most fortunate in acquiring life long male friends. I have had so many and still have that I am what one would call a 'lucky bunny'

One hears that the happiest days of ones life are their school days. True or not there is no doubt that my years at my Prep and Public School has had the greatest effect on my whole life.

I hope readers will find some items of interest in the book. There is no doubt that I spent my youth in the age between the two World Wars, which will never be repeated. It was a life without health & safety and political correctness. It mattered whom your parents were as one expected to follow in their fathers footsteps and follow that procedure. There was then very few exceptions to the rule. I myself was extremely fortunate to be born to an upper middle class family. It was an age of privilege compared to the trials and tribulations of the working class.

Great pleasure has been derived in preparing these memoirs as this has resulted in tracing my best friend's daughter, Jenny and the son and daughter of the woman I loved best, John and Lelia. The three have become great friends of mine.

An extraordinary thing happened in 2009 when I received a telephone call from South Africa to say I had a cousin aged 86 years. This was entirely out of the blue as my aunt Winifred had given birth to an illegitimate girl in 1923. In those days this was unthinkable and Joan was boarded out away from Avening House and eventually shipped to an affluent family in South Africa. Joan did not find out her identity until the day before her wedding to a barrister in Cape Town named Herb McKenzie. The McKenzie's had six children who now live around the World.

It was a great delight that suddenly I had a cousin who appeared from nowhere. In fact I met Joan and five of her relations in October 2009 when they attended the Farmiloe Reunion. I have also met two other of her sons and look forward to further visits.

On a personal note to finish I would be delighted to have letters or emails from readers and would do my best to respond personally.

Douglas Farmiloe

Henstead Hall, Church Road, Henstead,

Suffolk NR34 7LD

g.d.farmiloe@btconnect.com

ACKNOWLEDGEMENTS

I was fortunate when I first met Patrick Streeter who was the Archivist and old boy at my Prep School, Heath Mount. I had informed him that I was writing my memoirs of Heath Mount. He published a booklet I wrote called 'A Memoir of a Hampstead Schoolboy' which has been incorporated in the Heath Mount section.

Once again I was fortunate when I mentioned to him that I was writing my memoirs. He took on board this new venture as Editor as a labour of love with expenses only. Thanks Patrick. My thanks also to James Barraclough another old boy of Heath Mount who has kindly helped proof read my memoirs. I have also had considerable support from Uppingham with special thanks to Jerry Rudman, the Archivist there.

Would also like to thank numerous friends of mine who have bravely put up with reading my chapters of the Memoirs as they appeared. My thanks to Philip Clifford, a close friend of my son, and has enthusiastically read my draft of the book and made suggestions to possible changes.

Also my thanks to Tim and Andrew Farmiloe, for their helpful information on the early part of the Farmiloe History. Thanks also to Sally Farmiloe for her encouragement to this mammoth task.

Fortunately I have in my possession numerous photographs of which some are reproduced in the book. However I am grateful to those who have provided some missing pictures, which are also reproduced in this book.

My greatest encouragement has come from my friend Jacqui, to whom I am dedicating this memoir. She has spent a massive amount of hours, reading and then rereading my awful writing to type the memoirs and then point out mistakes and omissions until the finished edition is completed. Hours have been spent on the Internet checking up details and real detective work in tracing the daughter of my greatest friend Neville Southwell and then after hours tracing the son and daughter of Aliki.

There are quotes in the book from two authors. Stephen Fry has kindly allowed this from his book 'Moab is my Washpot' I have also quoted from 'By Gods Grace' a history of Uppingham school by Bryan Matthews. I feel sure that Bryan who died in 1987 would have given his permission had he been alive today. Bryan was the archetype of Uppingham School, being a boy there, as well as headmaster, librarian and archivist. I knew Bryan as he was at school with me and he actually visited me at Henstead Hall.

CONTENTS

Family Tree

Paternal

Grandparents   Thomas Meakin Farmiloe   (m)   Fanny Elizabeth Farmiloe (Budgie)

1857-1930   1861-1960

George Frederick	Howard	Edgar	Douglas	Margaret	Winifred	Alaric
(1885-1917)				(1894- 1954)	(1896-1970)	(1900-1963)
(Killed in Action)	(m) Audrey			(m) Robert Lee	Joan Mckenzie	
					(b)1923	
(m) Doris Rose Kingsley	Jack Jill			Tom John Rosemary		
				(b) 1933 (1935-2006) (1938-1991)		

George Douglas

Married (1) Ivy Katherine (Pat) Cotton   Married (2) Dorothy Ashby

---

George Michael	Susan Elizabeth		Shirley
(b) 1939	(b) 1944		(1942-2003)

Richard	Charles	Lewis	Sheba (b) 1959	Bo Michael (b) 1970
(15 Great Grandchildren)				

Helen (b) 1975

Family Tree

Maternal

Grandparents   George Kingsley   (m)   Rose Alice Graham

|

| | |
Doris Rose Jane   Shirley   Douglas

(m1)   (m)   (m)

George Frederick (1914)   Lois   Vera

| | |

George Douglas   David Joan Diana   Ian

(m2)

Edward Colman

CHAPTER ONE

Origins

The Farmiloe family originated from the cluster of villages around Minchinampton, Horsley and Avening, just outside Stroud in Gloucestershire. The name is probably a combination of Faeman, a personal name, and the Old English word, hlaew, meaning a hill. The first patriarch was William Farmiloe who was born in 1725 and was the local schoolmaster, as well as Parish Clerk and Clerk to the Vestry. His son, also William was born in 1766 and in 1793 we find him living in Clerkenwell, London, pursuing the trade of watchmaker, a bad time to follow this occupation as in 1797 William Pitt put a tax on clocks and watches to help pay for the Napoleonic Wars. The name Clerkenwell comes from the ancient practice of the Parish Clerks of London performing sacred plays around a well. A tablet once marking this spot is now in the wall of the Parish Church, St. James'. The well chamber is within the new offices of The New Statesman. William died insolvent; aged only forty in 1806 and this melancholy event was followed four months later by the suicide by hanging of his wife, Ury. Four children were left, aged 13, 10, 8 and 7, who were looked after by William's sister, Anne. We are most interested in George, the youngest. He was educated at the Parish School to the age of twelve. Reputedly his uncle George Western, Anne's husband lent him £25 to start in business and by 1823 he had set himself up as a builder's merchant at 34 St. John Street, Clerkenwell. His business prospered embracing the sale and manufacture of sanitary appliances, lead sheet and pipe, stained-glass windows, leaded lights, brass work, metal casements, paint, putty, oil, turpentine, varnish and glazing work. We get a snapshot of George from the 1841 census which lists him, aged 42, living at 114 St. John Street, with his wife, Elizabeth two servants and six sons, Thomas, 15, William, 13, Lewis, 7, Henry, 5, James, 3 and John, 1. I mentioned that William from Minchinhampton was the patriarch of the family but perhaps this title might be more properly held by George who established the clan and founded its prosperity. He built the fine building at 34 St. John Street, which still stands. It replaced an earlier one destroyed by fire in 1866; such was the conflagration that the molten stock of lead and glass fused into one common mass. Captain Shaw, of Gilbert and Sullivan fame, with twelve engines and 68 firemen, attended the blaze. The business moved to Mitcham in 1999. The building is now owned by his descendent, Tim Farmiloe. Much of the old interior survives and it is now used for film locations and photo shoots.

George's wife, Elizabeth Meakin, came from a family of successful

Staffordshire potters and a number of Farmiloe's married Meakin's, also Farmiloe's married other Farmiloe's. In consequence I have far fewer ancestors than the possible quota. The family were prone to inherited diseases from this interbreeding and after a while there was active discouragement of cousins marrying. In my time James Farmiloe wished to marry his cousin Grace Rees but the engagement was blocked. Poor Grace never married and shared her life with a large poodle.

My great-grandfather, another George, the second son, was born in 1826. He joined the family business and, besides being a founder-member of the London Metal Exchange, was responsible with his father for the business's great expansion during the periods of Victorian prosperity. He was the first to establish the family's connection with Hampstead, living at 43 Maresfield Gardens in the late 1880s. His interests outside business included cricket and he was President of his own club. In 1897 the business became a limited company, George Farmiloe & Sons Ltd. George, and his son, Thomas Meakin Farmiloe, my grandfather, were the largest shareholders. George died in 1906 leaving £120,000, about £7 Million in 2010 values. My grandfather, Thomas, together with his cousin, James, and later my father George and his brother Howard, continued to run the business.

CHAPTER TWO

Early Days

I was born on 22nd March 1915 and given the first name George, so that I could become the fifth generation with that name. My grandfather nicknamed me Quintus. I was lucky to avoid the sobriquet Sextus, who I recall from the classics was a notorious rapist. For those unaware of the poem 'Horatius' by Babbington Maccauley, which went as follows:

But when the face of Sextus was seen among the foes,

A yell that rent the firmament from all the town arose.

On the housetops was no woman but spat towards him and hissed,

No child but screamed out curses and shook its little fist.

My second name, Douglas, came from my father's brother-in-law of whom he was particularly fond. I only discovered this a few years back when this Douglas, then aged 93, told me. Although I had the first name George I was usually called Douglas, but some people today call me George.

Can people remember events when they were two or three? Or are they imagining things or remembering what they were told? My first memory, when I was 2 ½, is of an air raid in 1917 when a Zeppelin flew over London. My mother took me down to the basement of the flats at the top of Hampstead High Street. A little while later we lived in Jersey for about six months where I attended my first school. I recall little except playing on the sands and climbing some marvellous rocks. My father was killed in the First World War while serving in the Honourable Artillery Company at the Battle of Bullencourt, he was killed on the 26th June 1917 aged 31 and is buried at the Mory Abbey Cemetery, north of Bapaume. He was born in 1885 and was the eldest of the family and like me he attended Heath Mount School, and then went to West Downs in Winchester, before going on to Uppingham in 1899. He finished his education at Trinity Hall, Cambridge. I have some letters from him to my grandmother sent between 1905 and 1907 from Belgium and Frankfurt, Germany. He was there to learn languages and also taught hockey to German ladies, a game he was particularly good at. Fishing was a passion of his and although abroad he regularly read The Fishing Gazette. His sense of humour comes through in these letters. While waiting with friends in Brussels for a train he amused himself on roundabouts and in a cake shop.

While in Frankfurt he went to the opera to see The Geisha and complained about the size of the German lady opera singers, 18 stone with three-yard waists and totally inappropriate to play svelte Japanese girls. Also his clothes caused a sensation. The Germans could not get used to his Norfolk jacket with flannel collar and stared at him as if he was a freak. When he wore his Uppingham blazer at a hockey match they thought he was the advance party of a circus and gave him a good cheer.

Back in England in the census of 1911, then aged 25, he signed the form as Head of the Household, presumably because his parents were away on holiday. He gave his occupation as clerk with Lead and Glass Merchants. We would now call a clerk a junior manager and he was working for Farmiloe's. I was two years old when my father died. I have a letter that Budgie, my grandmother, wrote to him in June of that year that is particularly evocative, particularly as it was returned after he had been killed. It is a cheerful, chatty letter, full of wartime news. His brother Howard had been promoted to Captain in the London Regiment and was later mentioned in dispatches. A friend's office had been bombed out and the occupants had a lucky escape. Teader, the coachman had been called up and the cricket matches at Hampstead had been interrupted by thunderstorms.

After his death my mother had a romance with a Spaniard. I do not recall him but she said he had perfect manners. Then she met and married my cruel stepfather Edward (Eddie) Colman. They lived for a while in Willoughby Road, Hampstead and later moved to Brussels. (A neighbour of ours in Willoughby Road was a little girl called Anne Buchanan. I never met her at the time but ninety years later I annually complete her tax return). I recall little of my life in Brussels. There is a photo of me with a scooter by a large stone lion. Our flat was in Avenue de Cortenberg. I loved going to the woods on the outskirts of the city. In 1983 my wife and I visited them again and after sixty years they brought back vivid memories of childhood. Eddie was a cousin of Ronald Coleman the actor and he and I did not get on. The marriage only lasted two years although my mother kept his name for the rest of her life. When living in Brussels he was cruel to her and relations between them became so bad that my maternal grandmother and great aunt Lily had to come over and rescue me.

My next home was in Great Holland, near Frinton-on-Sea in Essex. The village, which is still unchanged today, consisted of two roads, which joined at the Ship Inn. Next to the inn were two workman's cottages. At first we stayed in the inn and the landlord was Frank Reed and my mother, who I always knew as Dodie, had been a friend of his family for some time. His daughter Elsie had worked for her and the two were lifelong friends. I recall playing in the Public Bar and a delightful rose garden at the back. We then moved into one of the cottages. Mr Sadler, the baker, lived next door and I would play with his son. Across the road was the baker's shop next door to Mr Crampin's post office and grocery. I recall two particular characters from the village. Firstly Walter Green, the farmer at Manor Farm; he was always dressed as an Edwardian Gentleman, very upright with a grey moustache, brown suit and bowler hat and a walking stick. He would drive up and down the village in his pony and trap. The other was Mrs Travers of Great Holland Lodge. She was very Victorian and always dressed in black with her collar up to her chin. Like Mr Green she drove around in a pony and trap. I went to a small private school about a mile away, accompanied on the bus by a young girl of about seventeen, who was also a pupil.

Frinton, then, as now, was a very genteel seaside town. By road it was about four to five miles away and the bus was not allowed into the town but stopped at the far side of the railway crossing; but you could walk there along a mile long track and footpath. While at the Ship Inn, although only seven or eight, I had my first date. There was a beautiful young lady of about twenty-five staying there. I was enraptured and saved up my pocket money to take her to the cinema and my invitation was sportingly accepted. The night before I went to bed fully dressed so as to be ready in the morning but my mother found out and I had to revert to my pyjamas. No doubt my date paid for the cinema and tea at Clacton but I hope my pocket money covered my half-fare on the bus. I also recall the Bug family and their many children who lived on the right hand side of the lane on the way to Frinton. One daughter, Edie was about my age and we played together a lot and she was the first girl I kissed, but my mother would get very annoyed because I was playing with working-class children. People were more snobbish then. My grandmother, a true Victorian, would take the same view when my wife's daughter Shirley played with those of the gardener.

My grandparent's home was Avening House, Arkwright Road, Hampstead. It was a fine mansion set on the corner with Ellerdale Avenue. Sir Thomas Beecham, the conductor and Sir Reginald Bloomfield, the architect lived opposite and my grandparents knew them both. The house had four to five acres of grounds, more than its neighbours, and encompassed a kitchen garden, greenhouse, garage with a flat, studio, stables and courtyard. The lower lawn was big enough for a cricket pitch. At the back was a large wall separating the property from the University College School. The house was sold in 1935 for £6,500 and nine nice houses built on the site. Each of these would command over £1 million now. I came to live at Avening House under their care at the age of nine. One might have thought that being an only child with no father and being pushed from pillar to post would have been unsettling. But it was not, I was always happy, loved and spoilt by all. One does not miss what one does not know.

The first two years with my grandparents, from the ages of nine to eleven, I was very much on my own and I had to find my own amusements. With the exception of snakes I loved animals. When about seven I recall visiting a friend of Dodie's in Streatham called Mrs Semina who had an Alsatian of which I became very fond and they have remained my favourite breed. None of my family were animal lovers, in fact Dodie had a phobia of cats, but both my wives were, one of the few things I had in common with them. At Avening House, below the flat of the coachman, Teader were some stables. Six horses once lived there but they had all gone by the time I arrived so I filled the vacuum with numerous animals. I had a few cats and dozens of rabbits of all shapes and sizes. The latter multiplied but I did not know why. I also had a number of birds bought in a pet shop in Camden Town. Once, when bringing a bird home on the train it escaped and flew up to the top of the roof at Camden Town station. Two very helpful porters rescued it with ladders, something that would not happen on today's tube – but this was 1924. I did not clean the animals out; this occupation was given to Teader, the redundant coachman. An earlier task of his was, when I was a baby, riding to Highgate to a farm to fetch milk for me. Once I brought a puppy back from the pet shop but my grandmother, reckoning a wayward grandson was bad enough without an unpredictable dog as well, made me return it.

At Avening House we would either visit or be visited by numerous great aunts. Both my father and grandfather were the eldest of their generation so the off spring of these great aunts were only some four to twelve years older than I, but the great aunts seemed to a boy of eight to be of a great age although they would have only been in their forties or fifties. Indeed these ladies had Victorian values and were very straight-laced. On the first-floor landing I devised a game of football that I could play by myself. The space provided a suitable rectangle and I placed chairs by the doors to act as goalkeepers, the ball having to go over the chair or through its legs to score. I carefully kept all the scores and my imaginary teams performed in the FA Cup, in all the Leagues plus the Isthmian and Athenian. There was a handicapping system to even out matches between First and Third Division teams. It was great fun and gave me a love of League Tables and knowledge of football. Sadly both my schools were rugby playing ones so my experience was wasted. To play rugby I would have had to involve one of the maids and she may not have approved of being tackled. No one objected to my football, grandfather was in the city, Budgie, my grandmother was downstairs or out, and I had hours of amusement. Off the landing was a billiard room with a full-sized table. In the corner were relics of the first war such as tin hats, shells and bayonets. I played many hours of billiards, keeping imaginary scores of the greats such as Joe Davis and the Australian Walter Lindrum. This practice stood me in good stead and I won the cup at my prep school, Heath Mount, beating Beaumont-Thomas in the final. Amazingly I also managed to play cricket by myself in the enclosed stable yard. The stables acted as a pavilion and two brick walls at the ends. A box acted as the wicket; I would bowl at the wall and then strike the ball with my bat as it bounced back. Again scores were kept; the teams would be Hampstead or Middlesex. I used to take tea breaks and repair to the eponymous Mrs Teader's flat above the stables. On other occasions I would get Teader to bowl to me on the lower lawn, which was the size of a proper pitch. Sometimes I would hit the ball over the wall and he would have to chase down the hill outside to retrieve it. Balls could travel a quarter of a mile down the Finchley Road, but luckily for the fielder they usually got stuck in the gutter. I luckily never hit a car or pedestrian.

I am afraid I got myself into much mischief. On one occasion I hid in a walnut tree with a can of dirty water and threw it over my grandfather, as he was about to get into his car to go to the city. He was furious and I was banished for the summer holidays to my cousins at Sandown Farm at Long Bridge Deveril in Wiltshire. Teader accompanied me on the train and I gave him the slip at Warminster. The poor man did not know where the farm was and arrived some hours after me. This banishment was no punishment as I enjoyed playing with my three cousins who were around my age. Muffie, one of them, and I would bring in the 28 cows and milk them. By the time she was thirteen she could run the farm but she abandoned it for the city life.

My grandparents were no doubt kind and lenient to me but I did learn discipline from my aunt Hilda who was in charge when they were away. One day she and Nurse Robinson decided I should go for a ride in the car with them driven by Chambers, the chauffeur. I wanted to play football on the landing and so locked myself in the lavatory, but Hilda got the better of me and locked the outside door as well. They went for their drive and I was incarcerated for three hours. Had my grandmother been there she would have given in. Another of my delinquencies was stealing food from the evening meal. Until I was eleven I did not join the adults for dinner; they ate at 8.30pm, my grandfather often did not return from his office until late. The maids, Madge and Ellen, served the meal from a hatch in the dining room after the backstairs staff had placed it there. In consequence there was a delay and I crept down the back stairs and, like a crafty fox, pinched some of the food for a feast in my room. The two maids knew what I was up to and turned a blind eye, and I suspect grandmother was in on the conspiracy as well.

From the age of eleven I had all the freedom I required and I was totally streetwise. Pocket money was ample; no one was concerned as long as Budgie knew where I was going and I returned in good time. I would catch a bus in Finchley Road, I can remember the numbers well, 2, 13 and 48, and go, perhaps to Madame Tussauds where the Chamber of Horrors was my favourite, or to the National History Museum in Kensington to see the Brontosaurus, or to Lord's Cricket Ground where, as grandfather was a member, I had a free pass to the pavilion. I saw every day of the 1926 Australian Test and can still remember the scores. Sometimes Grandfather came too and he once introduced me to my idol the celebrated Patsy Hendren. Other outings included the local cinemas; the Ionic at Golders Green or the Hampstead Playhouse where, for an extra three pence you had a cup of tea with biscuits. Often I ran home pretending I was Tom Mix, the celebrated cowboy. In fact Tom and his horse did come over from the States once to Hampstead Heath attracting great crowds. My cinema visits, usually on my own, included the West End where films ran for nine months before visiting the suburbs and provinces; The Leicester Square, The Empire and The Tivoli in the Strand were my haunts. No harm ever came of me but not many of today's children will have this freedom.

As soon as I went to Heath Mount I made many friends; after school we would visit each other's houses for tea. On one occasion my intended friend could not come and I had difficulty in finding a substitute, finally asking Harry Watts, the elder brother of my contemporary Jack. Harry was six foot tall and older than me and I was short for my age so we made an incongruous couple. Arriving at home I said to Budgie, 'this is Harry Watts. I couldn't get anyone else.' She reprimanded me for my rudeness but Harry took no offence.

My grandparents had eight children but three of them were haemophiliacs; Douglas died as a teenager and Edgar, a talented painter, died in his twenties but I do not remember either of them. Hilda lived in the studio in the garden with a nurse to look after her. In later life she was wheelchair-bound and lost all her fingers, she wore mittens with just thumbs. Because of her indigestion all her food had to be mashed, but she liked a sherry and an occasional cigarette. She liked playing cards and was one of the bravest and most cheerful people one could meet. My other two aunts were Margaret and Winifred. I have no idea of life in a girl's public school but my grandfather sent both my aunts to Roedean, which was then, and still is one of the top public schools for girls. They shared a large bedroom next to mine; both were about thirty when I was growing up and were both attractive so it was surprising they were not married. They went to parties and were supposed to be back by a reasonable hour. On one occasion they were late and my grandfather was waiting for them with a stick and chased them up stairs. They rushed through my door and then quickly into their own room, locking the door after them.

Margaret went to Canada for a holiday and met a farmer there who she married. This did not go down well, as he was considered socially inferior. Had they settled down quietly things might have been alright but she paraded her farmer boy at parties in front of all the family, which was not appreciated. Eventually they moved to the Midlands and had three children; the two boys have always been close to me. She died quite young, before my grandmother. I was always very fond of her. Winifred should have married earlier. She was engaged to a dapper little man who was training to be a doctor but at the age of forty he still had not qualified. Eventually she married at sixty five, having passed her driving test at 64, and we waited for the baby to arrive at 66. A fortune teller told her of the family she would live the longest and she was right. Of the three remaining sons my father was killed in the Great War, Howard was married and Alaric lived at Henstead and I will speak of him later.

The first word I ever said to my grandmother was Budgie. Where this came from I will never know but it stuck and she has always been known as Budgie to me. Everyone else used that name when I was present and she used it when writing to me. Grandfather was 6ft tall and broad, she was 5ft and slim so my name for him became 'More Budgie.' My grandfather was the perfect example of a wealthy Victorian gentleman. When in London, until the day he died aged 73 in 1930 he went to his office in the city. He enjoyed life to the full, worked hard and played hard. He had a love of cricket, which I inherited, and he played for the MCC and Hampstead. Right up to his last summer after work he went to the nets at Hampstead to be bowled at by the professionals. Much to their annoyance he would arrive late in the evening when they were ready to go home and he was given the nickname, 'the Midnight Cricketer'. Golf was another passion and each March he would take my grandmother to Cannes to stay at the Hotel Beausite. He died on the golf course there playing a shot. Budgie had to bring his body back and it lay in state in the drawing room at Avening House. I recall it well as I had just come home from Uppingham for the school holidays. The impressive funeral procession took a considerable time to reach Highgate Cemetery and I have never witnessed so many Farmiloe's than at the huge reception at Avening House afterwards. Like many Victorian gentleman he ate heavily, three large meals a day plus a snack at tea, but he kept fit and had a cold bath or swim every morning. This bath was a ritual. The maid filled it up; on arrival he would eat an apple, then gaze at the Farmiloe family tree on the wall, which he had commissioned. Then he would get into the bath and splash the water all over the floor for the maid to clear up. Now refreshed he would shout at the top of his voice, whether they were there or not, everyone's names – Quintus for me, 2096, our telephone number, for Budgie, then he would open the beige door and shout for Nurse Robinson and the ritual was wound up with a healthy breakfast.

When we were in Southwold he would cycle down to the beach and I had to go with him. There were two fishermen with bathing huts, Smith and Palmer and he would patronise them alternatively. I never enjoyed these early morning dips but I did enjoy the breakfast afterwards; porridge, fish, bacon and eggs, and toast if there was room.

Grandfather was a great hoarder, a trait I have inherited and it has been useful in writing these memoirs. Every letter, receipt and document was kept and deposited in numerous desks around the house. After he died I enjoyed going through all these. Budgie cleared most of them out but some bundles survived and she took these down to Henstead. Also she kept many of his clothes and stored them in a room at the top of the house. When I moved in, there were suits, top hats, smoking jackets and caps as well as a walking stick, which I still use. Neither would he discard his cars. At the back of the garage was a Panhard. During the twenties he owned a Lancia. It had a collapsible hood and was draughty, even in summer, and Budgie had to wrap up well. Towards the end of the twenties this car was displaced by a Double Six Daimler, a large car with a special large chassis to accommodate Aunt Hilda's wheelchair. On being finally sold it spent its final days as a hearse in Lowestoft.

My grandfather was a proud man, a trait of the Victorian upper middle classes who were challenging the aristocracy. I recall once at a London railway station he was talking to Pat Corkery, the son of a seamstress who did work for us. Pat had his hands in his pockets and grandfather gave him a real dressing down. Incidentally after grandfather died Budgie sponsored Pat and paid for his training as an osteopath. He had a successful practice in Norwich but sadly died young. Grandfather had a full-length portrait painted which hung at the foot of the staircase at Henstead. When Dorothy, my second wife, and I moved in she had it rolled up and sadly it has not survived. Budgie's attitudes were similar. Servants were always called by their surnames and they addressed you as 'Sir' or 'Madam' and the female ones curtsied. I was brought up at the tail-end of this culture and am broadminded but I find it strange when Christian names are now always used, particularly in business. My grandfather's attitude to women was very Victorian. A wife was to look after the house, have children and to look attractive when they went out. Mistresses were for fun but I do not know if he had one; he was too busy. He would never consult his wife if he were going away to play golf, cricket or shoot. Every spring they went to the South of France and in the summer holidayed at Southwold. The Farmiloe's had a close bond with Southwold and he donated money for a trust for the Fisherman's Reading Room, which is still in existence. Because of this he was granted the freedom of Southwold in the 1920's. He was only the second man to receive the honour. He always sat in the front seat of the car next to Chambers, the chauffeur, while Budgie sat in the back. When the family went to church the men walked 50 yards ahead of the women. Even when my grandparents dined alone Budgie would leave the table when the meal was finished and he would sit there for an hour drinking port and smoking a cigar. Then he might go to the drawing room, where Budgie sat alone, exchange a few words, and go to bed. I have a letter from my grandfather to his sister, great aunt Popsy, complaining about his father's will and the difficulties he had in getting hold of the money. He wrote, 'I will not worry you with details because they would be beyond the intelligence of a woman'. Ironically he was just as bad with his own will. Budgie never had proper control of her own money and from what she did have she left a little to me.

At the reception after my grandmother's funeral I recall the Vicar saying to my aunt Winifred that Budgie was of a very strong character and must have ruled the family. Winifred replied, 'You didn't know my father.' But Budgie was of a strong character and led an active life independent of her husband. She was in complete charge of the house and servants. Each morning she would visit cook in the kitchen and she would write out on a blackboard the menus for the day. Once at dinner the maid had laid the cutlery incorrectly so she picked up the offending utensils and dropped them on the floor. The servants had an evening a week off but they had to be back by eleven. Budgie would check them in. Today this sounds draconian but Victorians were moralists and they acted for the common good. To be out after eleven meant only one thing. Temptation must be avoided.

Like us all Budgie had emotions but she was unable to express them. Once I recall her falling over in Oxford Street and a sympathetic crowd formed around to help her, but she was most annoyed by their interference. Her children were all brought up by nurses Mallard and Robinson, and so she had little involvement with them, affection was hidden and I never saw any of her children kiss her. Reading the letters between her and my father I can see the great love she had for him. He wrote when he was short of cash, directing the request via her to my grandfather. She kept all his letters including the sad one she wrote to him only for it to be returned with the news that he had been killed in action. She wrote to me every week during the second world war. She spoilt me when I visited Henstead; I liked oranges but was too lazy to peel them. She prepared them for me, removing both the pith and the pips. They tasted scrumptious and nobody has ever done this for me again. When I was short of cash she always sent me an allowance. I recall when Dorothy and I were running a toy shop one Christmas we overstocked and we asked her for a loan to pay our wholesalers. Dorothy insisted in giving her four post-dated cheques but, although she approved of Dorothy's actions, she tore them up. After our visits to Henstead she prepared food for us to take back, enough for two or three days; a joint or cooked chicken and my favourite, Fuller's cakes from the shop in Oulton Broad. They were made of sponge with chocolate or icing cover and a large walnut on top. Also included were cigars from the collection my grandfather left. On leaving Henstead I gave her a hug and a kiss and I can still see this frail old lady standing by the door until my car was out of site. She meant a great deal to me.

To finish this chapter I would like to say a word about the servants at Avening house. There were several gardeners to look after an acre of kitchen garden, a large green house, three lawns and numerous flower beds and paths. Four staff lived in, cook, a scullery maid called Alice who later moved to Henstead and married a man from Beccles, Madge, the housemaid and Ellen the parlour maid. Madge also moved to Beccles and later married the widowed chauffeur, Chambers. Tradesmen called at the side-door and sometimes there was a delay in answering them. One once left a note for his fellow tradesmen, 'Brother tradesmen do not weep. They are not dead but fast asleep'. Chambers was a good friend of the family. He was tall and had one finger missing. He lived in Hampstead in a flat with his wife and son and followed us down to Henstead. During the Second World War he and Madge looked after my son Michael for a while. They retired to Carlton Colville, Lowestoft.

CHAPTER THREE

Heath Mount

I entered Heath Mount in 1924 when I was nine and left four years later for Uppingham. I enjoyed the four years and the happy memories have always remained with me. The school was at the top of Heath Street, hence its name, and was situated at one of the highest points in London. My home, Avening House, gave good views all over London but it was not as high as the school. Nearby was the famous Whitestone Pond from whose shore Hampstead Heath extended. The heath separated the buildings of Hampstead from those of Highgate and an old sage, Mother Skipton, used to say that when this area was built over the end of the world would come. In the twenties the Heath was a regular spot for murders. We callous schoolboys would have great pleasure in finding the exact spot of the latest grisly deed.

My first Headmaster was J.S. Granville Grenfell. As I was, at first, a dayboy our paths did not very often cross. He was then sixty and appeared a very old, distant character and my main memory of him was, in my first year, lining up with all the school to bid him goodbye on his retirement. He had been in ill health for some time, attributed by him to overwork, and he retired to Cimiez, France where he died two years later. The Deputy Head, Mr Scotsman, had been acting in for him for a while. The new Head Master was the Reverend A.R.K.Wells –nicknamed Ark.

My father left Heath Mount in 1897 to go to West Downs Prep School for two years before proceeding to Uppingham. His Head Master was also Mr Grenfell, then aged 33.

There were many imminent Old Boys before and during my time at the school.

Well documented was the bullying of Evelyn Waugh to Sir Cecil Beaton who both went to Heath Mount.

Another famous Old Boy was Sir Gerald Du Maurier the actor who died in 1934 (Heath Mount 1882-87). His father the author wrote Trilby and Gerald's daughter Daphne Du Maurier is well known for her novels such as Rebecca and Jamaica Inn. Others who became famous were Sir Arnold Bax, Master of the Kings Music and writer of a number of symphonies. John Lewis founder of the well known Departmental Store. My own era provided well known figures such as the classical composer Humphrey Searle, Peter Copley the actor and Ian Wallace for ever associated with Mud, Mud, Glorious Mud.

There was little bullying in my time. There was one small Jewish boy, nicknamed 'Ikey' who suffered. It was strange that he was picked out as, being in the cosmopolitan and prosperous area of Hampstead and Golders Green there were many Jewish and foreign pupils. One of my good friends, Peter Ginsberg was Jewish and he was very popular. (It was however rumoured that Peter's younger brother, Donald used to lend him money and charge interest).

In my day the school must have had about 75 pupils, all boys and about twelve were boarders. I boarded for my last year and, my home being so close, I often ran away, but I was always dispatched back to school. Before each lesson one boy stood by the door and, as soon as the master came along the corridor, the boy would rush ahead and shout, 'Cave', Latin for 'Watch Out.' Then all the pupils were supposed to sit down and be quiet. Right from the start one learned Latin. I have never forgotten what the Revd Wells taught me. I can still recite, 'A, ab, absque, coram, de, add, super, supter.' A fellow pupil, John Sherriff, was similarly taught as he recounted in a letter quoted in the Heath Mount Register. I think the Latin was of doubtful value but I will always be grateful for the Revd Wells drumming into me history dates. I knew the ones for every monarch and every battle. Today, at the age of 95, I can run them off – Marston Moor, 1644. Such information is invaluable in everyday life as I can place any old building or historical event into context. I believe such information is no longer taught in this way, which is a pity. There was however one date I could never remember, that of the Battle of Towton. Wells described it as 'a hoary old chestnut'. Today I can't recall it and am obliged to look it up – 1461.

Most of the boys lived within two or three miles from the school. It would take me about half an hour to walk from my home, Avening House, to school, less on the way back as it was downhill. Few boys used bicycles and, more often than not, we would entertain each other to tea.

The school had a large concrete playground which was unfit for organised games, so cricket, rugby, football and athletics took place on a sports ground five miles away. We were driven there by bus and there were cream buns and lemonade afterwards. Cricket was my favourite sport. In 1928, my father having been killed in the war, my 70- year-old grandfather played in the Father's Match. He was captain and, although scoring a duck, was so proud of my achievement that, that evening, he came to our dormitory and gave each boy sixpence. It was quite a lot then as 20 cigarettes were only 11.1/2d (just over 5p in today's money).

Boxing was a popular sport. Only two rounds of one and a half minutes were allowed. I note from my old copy of a Chronicle that I beat Dixon.

In my last year I boarded and, as there were only about a dozen of us, I found it at times boring, especially when it rained and we were inside. Set against this tedium two exciting trips stand out; one to the offices of The Daily Mirror in Fleet Street, where a fellow pupil's father would have worked; another to the Air Show at Croydon. We had much scope for indoor games; my favourites were chess and billiards. A fellow boarder, a Swedish boy called Uggla was an excellent chess player and invariably beat me. I did however vanquish him once in the final. Nigel Beaumont-Thomas, who was later killed in the War, was a fine billiards player, but I once beat him in a final thanks to a run of flukes. In the summer some nights, sometimes with, sometimes without permission, the boarders would have midnight feasts on the roof and one night, when there was a total eclipse of the moon, we slept up there.

Sunday night was bath night. 'Cleanliness is next to Godliness', the Revd Wells would say. For us dozen boarders there was one large bathroom containing four baths. At that time I could not understand why we did not have three sessions of four boys. Instead it was arranged that Harry Watts, who was six feet tall and had passed puberty, bathed alone. I later worked out that this was to prevent the smaller boys experiencing the trauma of witnessing a fully developed youth. In fact, by mistake, I did just this and indeed was traumatised!

Sex lessons in those days were unheard of, but the Revd Wells did make a stumbling and ineffectual attempt at them. In our last week at the school he would have the leavers individually into his study for a 'pep talk'. Here he would mention 'the sins of others' and 'the pitfalls of Public Schools' and the 'wickedness' of boys that were found there. Vague mention was made of 'rabbits', incidentally my nickname as I kept rabbits as pets, but after all this I was none the wiser, indeed just confused.

Displayed at the end of this chapter are two of my school reports, one when I was eleven and another when thirteen. The reader will notice that the second is much better which is a reflection of the improving abilities of the school.

Pupils were divided into five sections, Blue, Purple, Red, Yellow and mine, Brown. I understand that my section has now been disbanded. There were 'section marks' for PT, games, tidiness, punctuality and extras. A Prefect led the section and there was keen rivalry to win the Section Cup and avoid the Wooden Spoon. The prefect, who was also the Section Leader, was elected by the boys. All had a vote except the candidate. As soon as a vote was received by a candidate he left the room. In my last year I received the first vote but, as it turned out, it was the only one I got. I think it must have been Peter Southwell's; he was the younger brother of my best friend, Neville Southwell. Peter was unfortunate. He was very shy and greatly overshadowed by his elder brother. Sadly he died by his own hand in 1955. Neville was his parent's golden boy and shone in everything he did. No doubt if they had seen the consequences of their favouritism they would have acted otherwise. May I say another word about Mr Southwell? My father having been killed in the war, the three most important male influences on me were him, my grandfather, and the Revd Wells. Often I was around the Southwell's house; he was kind and caring and filled the gap left by my father. No words can be enough to thank him for seeing me through my early years.

One remarkable thing about my days at Heath Mount was, considering the school only had 75 boys, that it produced four MPs, all Conservatives, Derek Walker-Smith, a Minister of Health and later Lord Broxbourne, Henry Kirby, a very colourful man, John Wells, the son of the Headmaster who, in my time was just in a pram and, Peter Tapsell, who was first elected at the age of 29 and is still in the House 50 years later.

A word about the masters – I used to see the Revd Wells occasionally during the holidays. My fellow pupil, John Sherriff, described him as a disciplinarian, but he took a kindly interest in me and guided me through my fits of temper. John received 39 strokes of the cane one term but the record was held by Jack Watts, later an Harrovian, who received 45. Although no angel, I strangely, was never caned, although about six times I ran away to my grandmother's house at Avening House. Another great influence on me was General Stone, a lifelong friend of the Headmaster. He was in fact a Brigadier-General, the lowest rank for a General. He had had a very distinguished war record, seeing service in all the major campaigns of the Western Front and winning the DSO at the Battle of the Somme. He lived in the school and, as a boarder, I saw a lot of him. A keen cricketer, during quiet evenings and weekends he would bowl to us in the nets. On leaving Heath Mount he became Curator of Kenwood House, a mansion open to the public on the border between Highgate and Hampstead. When I needed a reference for an Army Commission I contacted him there. Another master for whom the boys had a great affection was Troughton Dean. He had a bad stutter and was devoted to Heath Mount, keeping in touch with all the Old Boys. He was the 'Mr Chips' of the school.

A mention of the boys – their parents were all well off. They had to be to afford the fees. Mr Van Zwannenberg had three sons to pay for. Some were titled and others millionaires, but there was no snobbery. We worked as a community and when not at school were in and out of each other's homes. I shall mention some individuals who were friends of mine. Nicholas Mavrogordato, a Greek boy; What ever happened to him? Hardinge Pritchard. He was given a pair of baby alligators called 'Ham' and 'Eggs' for a birthday present. I enjoyed seeing them when I went to tea there, but they grew too large and were given to the zoo. Alessio Domingo Robles, a Mexican boy who was only at the school for a few terms. He was very sunburnt and I envied him because we eleven-year-olds had to wear hated short trousers but he was allowed knickerbockers and long stockings, which covered his knees. We were close friends and I recall him saying that he wished we were blood brothers. He told us that his father was Governor of Mexico City. I recall my mother taking us both to The Tivoli cinema in the West End to see Charlie Chaplin in the silent film, The Gold Rush. A fine lunch and tea were included. Ian Jones was the son of the celebrated actor Sir Felix Aylmer. Ian was the best cricketer of his generation and was killed in the war. Paul Dixey became Chairman of Lloyd's. The picture in the Register of him reminds me of my great uncle Fred whose wife, Popsy, I named one of my goats after. Noel Arnold was a great friend of mine and he lived in picturesque Flask Walk. His mother was French and he had an elder brother, Roy who later emigrated to Canada. Noel later qualified as a solicitor. Joseph Fleming was a boy I could not get on friendly terms with. You could not exchange confidences with him. I mentioned that there was no bullying but he was an exception. He was six feet tall and weighed twelve stone and was teased because of his size. I felt sorry for him and twice went to his home in that secluded and select part of the Hampstead Heath called the Vale of Health. Thanks to his size he was a good Rugby player and he was also keen on cricket. In later years he was a familiar figure seen walking over the Heath. On the last occasion I saw Neville Southwell we were talking about old Heath Mount days and he said, 'Do you remember old Fleming. He was strange'. I recall that he coped well, in spite of the teasing, about his size and awkwardness; he clearly wanted to be liked and I hope my gesture of friendship made things easier for him. Each schoolboy has his bete noir and mine was Dixon. I regarded him as a squirt and, no doubt, the feeling was mutual. He is dead now; a Pilot Officer in the RAF he was killed on active service in April 1940. Dixon and I just did not get on. Was it because I beat him in the boxing final? We were taught to watch our opponent's eyes to see which way he was going to move. Such a tactic could make one look evil! He followed me to Uppingham and when we passed in the street we would just exchange grunts. Of the contemporaries I have mentioned four were killed in the war, Ian Jones, Lance Dixon, Harry Watts and Nigel Beaumont-Thomas. Lance Dixon did indeed die on active service but not in action. His mother married, for a second time, the Anglo-Italian novelist Rafael Sabatini and they lived at Hay-on-Wye, Herefordshire. As a young Pilot Officer, Lance flew his plane over the house at Hay to show off to his mother and stepfather. One wing tipped the ground and he crashed, killing himself in front of them.

He is buried in Hay on Wye cemetery.

Four of my Heath Mount friends remained as such in later life, Neville Southwell, Donald Gourlay, Peter Ginsberg and Roy Booth. Donald lived in a large house in Platts Lane. His father was the manager of a West End branch of Barclay's Bank. His mother was an Oetzmann, a family who owned a large London furnishing company, and was wealthy in her own right. Then they moved to Bryanston Court and became neighbours of Mrs Simpson, later the Duchess of Windsor. Whenever I got into trouble it was with Donald. At the age of twelve we would illicitly smoke in Perrins Court, the little alley connecting High and Heath Streets. Once we speculated where babies might come from. There was an old retired Victorian nurse, nurse Robinson who lived in a top floor flat in Avening House. An aged spinster, well into her seventies, she gave an explanation, mentioning the odd bird and bee, and as about as unhelpful as that produced by the Revd Wells. It was with Donald that, for the only time I was guilty of theft. My grandparent's house contained thousands of books, some valuable. We were short of money and considered that one or two would not be missed. We took six volumes to a book dealer in Hampstead and sold them, but we were spotted by one of the maids and grandfather sent his chauffeur to buy them back. He was a kindly man and never punished me. Donald also introduced me to housebreaking. He had left Charterhouse, my grandfather had died and my grandmother had moved to Suffolk. Avening House, where we had lived, was all boarded up ready for development. We broke in and roamed around the deserted rooms so full of memories. A sad occasion as it was shortly bulldozed down to make way for nine new houses. There is no more mournful sight than an old family home, all full of memories, empty and awaiting demolition.

As young men in the thirties Donald and I were habitués of the West End nightclubs – The Nineteenth, The Paradise, The Coconut Grove. We were once at such a place in Regent Street, amazingly in those days one could park outside the club all night without trouble. But on this occasion I must have parked my Jaguar on a bus stop and, on leaving the club at six am I could not find it. In fact the police had impounded it and it could not be collected until the next day. Donald told me he could make his own way home and that I could borrow his Bentley. In those days, stupidly, we had no inhibitions about driving and drinking. While tipsy I could manage my own car but not Donald's big beast and before long I had wrapped it around a bollard. I never saw Donald after 1938. At the outbreak of war I saw a picture of him in the paper in uniform preparing for action. Next I heard he had been cashiered. To his credit he then rejoined as a Private and subsequently regained a Commission. He emigrated to Canada after the war but in 1951 caught a bug and died aged thirty-five.

Peter Ginsberg was a different character to Donald. He, Neville Southwell and I shared a fanatical interest in Cricket. I fell in love with an exchange student from Denmark who was staying with the Ginsberg's. A sweet blond girl, we went out a number of times and wrote to each other after she returned to her hometown of Aarhus. Sadly distance caused love to fade. Peter came to stay with me at Henstead Hall, Suffolk. On a trip to see friends we had 'one over the eight'. Cars were few and there were no drink driving laws. I drove a small sports car, a Singer Le Mans and I failed to take a corner on the A12. We ended up side down in a field. I was thrown clear and Peter just bruised and without his watch. The next morning my grandmother's chauffeur, Chambers, announced that, 'Unless Master Douglas drives again quickly he may lose his nerve.' My grandmother instructed him to buy a slower car, a Triumph Gloria. It was too slow for me so back in London I bought a British Salmson. Readers will be glad to hear that I graduated to Rolls-Royces, gave up driving like Mr Toad and, for many years now, have strictly followed the drink driving laws.

MY GREATEST FRIEND

DR NEVILLE SOUTHWELL 1915-1992

I have been blessed during my stay on this earth in having two life long friends, Neville Southwell and Fred Tordoff (Uppingham). The accolade of best has to go to the former. Their paths rarely crossed. Obviously they were both present at my 21st Birthday Party at the Mayfair. The only other times were on the occasional guest appearance by Fred in a cricket team I ran called the Heathens.

I have outlived both. Neville was three months younger than me and arrived at Heath Mount after I went there. There was a soccer match between ourselves at the school and nobody wanted to play in goal. Poor Neville being a new boy had no chance and was put in goal. A position he had never played before and had little idea what to do. He conceded eight goals in the match and I think I scored about half of these. I felt sorry for him and after the match commiserated with him. That was the start of our great friendship.

The place I went to most was 17 Greenaway Gardens were the Southwell's lived. As my Father was killed in the First World War the Southwell's took a special interest in me. I still remember the house so well and the large top room was turned into a games room, which included a ¾ size Billiard Table. I spent many hours there playing with Neville and his younger brother Peter.

The Southwell's employed a young lady called Miss Scarlett whom I remember very well. She would have been in her early twenties and great fun. She was there to look after and amuse the two boys primarily Peter who was about 3-4 years younger than Neville. Many years later a young newly qualified Doctor called on Neville and said to him. You don't know me Sir, but my mother was a Miss Scarlett. Neville was so surprised that he immediately thought of me and telephoned me. I would then have been the only one alive who would have known her.

Even after I went to Uppingham and Neville went to Oundle the Southwell's continued their great kindness to me. When they visited Neville at Oundle they used to call at Uppingham and pick me up to see Neville. When they rented a large house near Saxmundham in Suffolk for the summer holidays I spent most of the time there with them.

Heath Mount only took twelve boarders and for my last year I became a boarder, as did Neville. Of course we had to have the beds next to each other so we could chat at night after lights were out.

1933-39

We saw a lot of each other after we left school until the outbreak of War. Neville went up to Cambridge and he used to ask me to their famous May Balls, which included on one visit to bring up as many girls in my car as I could due to the paucity of these (described in my memoirs). When Neville was in London we often went out to clubs and night clubs.

Of course he was occupied for a time with medical studies. Neville suffered badly from hay fever and he always told me one of the reasons he went into the Medical Profession was to find a cure for this. Then, of course, he had the perfect bedside manner to be a doctor.

Obviously I didn't see too much of Neville during the War as he was working in the hospital and I was stationed elsewhere. I did visit him at Brompton Hospital once and I stayed the night there with the other Doctors and had a few drinks and a chat. We corresponded regularly during the War and I still have in my possession some of the letters written to me during the War years informing me of what our mutual friends were doing during the War. Another lengthy letter told me all about his Wedding in 1941 and where he went on his honeymoon. Unfortunately I was stationed up North and could not get leave for the occasion. A further letter written in 1943: " I enjoyed our little drink together, especially as it was some time since we both met and really I think you are one of my oldest friends if not the oldest! How strange that you should have met Rene. I expect it did make you feel a little peculiar! After all you were pretty gay in those days and I don't think future generations will ever know London night life as it was in the years before this War. Rene wasn't really a bad little creature, I always rather liked her"

<u>1949-1992</u>

We had been the closest of friends for a quarter of a Century but now had families of our own and living in different parts of the Country so it was natural with different locations that we would not see each other to the same extent as previously.

I suppose in all we did meet more than a dozen times during this period but when we did they were great occasions. Sometimes he would call unexpectedly at Henstead Hall. I recall once after he had been very ill with heart trouble he praised Elizabeth his wife who nursed him so well through his illness.

I only called twice at Wyndham Croft, Turners Hill, Crawley, which, was his last home. The first time he was out when my wife and I called but Wally the gardener said I would find him at the pub. We went in for a drink and asked the barman if Dr Southwell was there. Neville was in the other bar but heard me ask for him. He immediately said before he saw me "I would know that voice anywhere in the World".

Neville who would have been so proud to know that his grandson Hugo Southwell has been the regular full back for Scotland rugby since 2007.

Farewell to a very dear Friend!

The Heathens

I would like to mention a team I used to organise. It was in 1937 that I had a rush of blood to the head and decided to form a sports club and in fact this led later to the organising of some sixty reunions of one type or another. I started off with a clean sheet, no ground, no players, no finances. The ground problem was easily solved, we were to be nomads and squat on other people's grounds. Then I needed a name; we were based in Hampstead, so from the Heath evolved the name The Heathens, and this was handy for my friends from my old Prep School, Heath Mount. Next we needed stars, and here

Uppingham and my old house, The Hall was useful. These stars were the Presidents and for rugby I chose Douglas Kendrew, my house captain for my early few terms, who had played for England shortly after he left school and later became captain. For cricket I found A.P.F.Chapman. He was before my time at school but his legend had lived on and he had been chosen to captain England in 1926. This blond-haired, gentle giant, with good looks and happy-go-lucky attitude caught the imagination of the country. With these two adornments it was easy to arrange fixtures. I do not know if the other players expected Kendrew and Chapman to play but their allure certainly brought people in.

Our record was good for the two years we were running and we were never disgraced. Neville Southwell used to bring down a car full of hefty undergraduates from Cambridge. If we could not make up the fifteen we would borrow a couple from the other side's reserves. Neville always had a good excuse for a shortage; perhaps there was a wedding and players had to go and celebrate. One match I remember was against the Metropolitan Police. It may have been their first team and the results were written up in the Stop Press section of the London Evening Standard. Heath Mount boys were relied upon to man the cricket team. Fred Tordoff also joined in as well as A.D.Newcombe, who played for Warwickshire 2nd XI. John Sherriff, an Old Heath Mountaineer persuaded V.F.Valli to play, a good bat from Westminster School but, in fact, neither of these two lived up to their promise.

HEATH MOUNT, HAMPSTEAD, N.W. 3.

NEXT TERM begins on *Sep 21*

Farmiloe's Report for _Summer_ Term, 192 _6_.

Age _11.4_ Form _IV_ His position in Form _10_. No. of Boys in Form _10_.

Note.—In deciding a boy's position in form the term's marks count two-thirds, and the examination marks one-third of the total.

THIS GRAPH SHOWS THE BOY'S POSITION WEEK BY WEEK DURING THE PAST TERM.

FORM MASTER'S REMARKS.

He has a fairly good memory but must learn how to write down his knowledge.

H. C. J. Hale

HEAD MASTER'S REMARKS.

An exceedingly nice plucky boy, of such an excellent sort that I am anxious to see him do well. But, if he is to do so, he must work just as hard as he possibly can, so as to catch up the average boy of his age. A. H. W.

	Place by Term's Work.	Place by Exams.	
LATIN	8	10	Is very weak in this subject. He seems quite unable to remember what he has learnt. Cd
FRENCH	10	10	Very backward indeed for his age at the beginning of term but his work has improved after Exam.
MATHEMATICS	10	10	ARITHMETIC 9 ⎫
			ALGEBRA 8 ⎬ He tries and will no doubt improve. H. C. J. H.
			GEOMETRY 10 ⎭
			~~TRIGONOMETRY~~
GERMAN, GREEK, or SCIENCE			
DIVINITY	10	2	Fair. His preparation is not well done. H. C. J. H.
GEOGRAPHY	3	7	Good. A very keen & interested worker. G.T.D.
HISTORY	7	3	Very fair. Works well but is slow to learn. W. G. Ch.
ENGLISH	10	10	Bad. Should read more good English. H. C. J. H.

Douglas' Report for 1926

HEATH MOUNT, HAMPSTEAD, N.W. 3.

Farmiloe _____ 's Report for Summer Term, 192 8

Age 13.4 _____ Form V His position in Form 7 No. of Boys in Form 14

Note.—In deciding a boy's position in form the term's marks count two-thirds, and the examination marks one-third of the total.

THIS GRAPH SHOWS THE BOY'S POSITION WEEK BY WEEK DURING THE PAST TERM.	FORM MASTER'S REMARKS.
	Has improved a good deal.

FORM MASTER'S REMARKS.

Has improved a good deal.

HEAD MASTER'S REMARKS.

A deeply affectionate boy who will take life rather hardly. He must learn to exercise self-control. He loses his temper far too easily in the playground None the less he is popular with the other boys. Sorry to lose him. A.D.W.

	Place by Term's Work.	Place by Exams.	
LATIN	7	2	Greatly improved.
FRENCH	8	7	Slow but definite improvement A.D.W.
MATHEMATICS	10	10	ARITHMETIC V. fair
			ALGEBRA Weak
			GEOMETRY Distinctly weak and careless. A.H.R
			TRIGONOMETRY
GERMAN, GREEK, or SCIENCE			
DIVINITY	2	4=	Good A.b.F.?
GEOGRAPHY	7	6	Good. He has made good progress. G.D.T.?
HISTORY	1	1	Easily his best subject. A.D.W.
ENGLISH	3	2=	Works hard and has improved considerably. A.M.

Douglas' Report for 1928

CHAPTER FOUR

Uppingham

My first term at Uppingham was without doubt the unhappiest three months of my life. I was totally unprepared for being away from home and thrown in with a complete set of strangers. I knew no one there and the discipline of a boarding school is harsh. I was short for my age, which did not help, and although not bullied I was put upon. Fagging was unpleasant. One was at the beck and call of the prefects, known as 'Polly's', at all times. You had to listen out for the call, 'Fag', drop everything and run to the caller. The last one to arrive undertook the task. To ignore the call meant six of the best. I was unprepared for all this. I had no siblings to confide in, my father had been killed in the war when I was two and I had had an unpleasant step-father. Up to the age of nine I rotated between my mother and two sets of grandparents and then I settled at Avening House. I was happy with this but it was no training for Uppingham. I boarded for the last year at Heath Mount, my grandparents thinking this was good preparation, but home was a quarter of an hour away, there were only twelve boarders and we were all friends. I often wonder how my father coped with Uppingham in his first term, but then his parents sent him to a boarding prep school for two years in preparation.

I sought to resolve my difficulties by running away. My house, The Hall, was isolated from the rest of the school, perhaps for this reason it was closed in 1993, and my escape required an early start. Perhaps I should have headed south to avoid the town but I recall Chambers, our chauffeur, coming into Uppingham from Kettering in the west. So I set off this way through the town and up Scale Hill, where the four Hill Houses were. I was wearing slippers as our shoes were kept in the changing room overnight for cleaning, and with no boater, but my early start meant I avoided 160 boys and four masters from the four Hill Houses. I had to be out by 6 am as the town became busy by 7am with roll call at 7.30am. My departure went smoothly and I was clear of Uppingham by the time I was missed. Kettering was fourteen miles away and some journey in slippers. There were few vehicles about and when I heard one I hid in a hedge. Later on, near Rockingham village, there was no cover and hiding was more difficult. I later heard that a number of masters had been searching for me so my hedge-hopping paid off. Eventually I reached Kettering where I found a garage and ordered a car to take me to London. The proprietor, alerted by my clothes was suspicious. He delayed me by preparing an enormous breakfast, for which I was most grateful. Then he telephoned the school and a master turned up, captured me, and drove back. Twenty five years later I was in the Falcon Hotel, Uppingham, with Tom Staples, whom I will introduce later, and I met the proprietor again and repaid his hospitality by buying him a large drink.

I was not punished at all for my escapade. It was the first time it had happened and the school did not know how to deal with the situation. I was given three days off and put in the private wing of the House to sleep. I learnt later that a year earlier a boy with polio had slept there and he had died and the whole house was shut down for the rest of term. I had my meals in matron's room and was told stories about the house and the times when Percy Chapman, the England cricket captain was there just after the war. I particularly remember making toast with matron in her room. There were no electric toasters and you used a very long fork, holding the bread over the fire. How much better it tasted then! I was very fond of Mrs Woodcock, the matron, and always visited her when I returned to Uppingham. Major and Mrs Shea, the Housemaster and his wife were very considerate and I gradually resumed school life. However I was still homesick and although I lived with my grandparents it was my mother who came and visited me. She came about four times a term and it was a strain on her finances as she stayed in the Central Hotel, now the Garden Hotel. She was now divorced from Eddie Colman and had little money. My grandfather had provided for her well when my father was killed but on remarrying she lost 80% of this, which reverted to me when I was 21.

My second term was the spring one, the shortest, from January to early April. I was no longer homesick and settled down to school life. My mother reduced the number of her visits and occasionally my grandparents came. During my last two years I never had a visit except when Mr and Mrs Southwell came and we visited Neville at nearby Oundle,

Certainly in my first term I lacked friends. There was a pecking order and you could not approach a boy senior to you unless he spoke to you. In my first term, besides me, there were four new boys in The Hall, Brian Bromley, Brian Douglas who was a gifted musician, Ernest English and Percy Kennedy. I have added Christian names but we would always refer to each other by surnames only. With the first three there was mutual toleration but in Percy I had a good friend and we still see each other – more of Percy later. In one way I was looking forward to the second term as I would rise in the pecking order. Only two boys were in the new intake, Fred Tordoff and Sam Watkinson, both from Yorkshire. Neither experienced the traumas I did, perhaps because they were cousins and Fred had an elder brother in the school. One did come across boys in other houses but the scope for friendships was limited. I can recall just two, Vernon Kirwan and John de la Hay, who later changed his name to Craufurd-Stewart. So remote were boys in other houses that I never met Ferdinand Eiloart whose father was a contemporary of my father's and who often appeared in his photo albums.

On the last day of the second term there was a rather unpleasant House event. The Fags had to complete the school steeplechase course. Behind us were the Polly's menacingly urging us on. The runners got soaking wet and no doubt caught colds for the holidays. On my first run I came equal last but we were both told we showed great pluck. I mentioned this barbaric ritual in my speech at The Hall reunion in 2007 but Percy Kennedy could not remember it at all. I think he must have left a day early to get back home to Dublin. In those days he must have spent hours on trains travelling back and forth.

I had a bad start to my first cricket term, which ruined any chances of my reaching the First XI. Although a reasonable bowler, batting was my strength and I had received my cricket colours at Heath Mount and had lessons at Lords. At the start of each term your ability was tested by the senior boys. There were 120 in our intake including A.F.T. White who captained Worcestershire in 1947/48. One only had ten minutes batting to show ones worth and I was determined to stay put and not lose my wicket. In fact I stonewalled, showing no adventure and scored just six in singles. This caution did not impress and I was disastrously confined to playing league cricket among the 'rabbits' and never received any coaching. In the five seasons at Uppingham I probably scored more runs for my house than anyone else in league cricket, but this was not as good as being in the XI.

A word more about fagging, one had to answer the Polly's call or there was a certain beating. The only excuse was to claim you were in the toilet. On one occasion I was with Percy Kennedy in his study and we were involved in setting up a business. There was a little shop adjacent The Hall, a converted front room run by 'Ma Weed' who sold sweets and milk shakes, for which she was famous. Bailey's the chemist also sold these but they were not as good. You would never find the recipe today. It involved essence - strawberry, raspberry or lemon - added to a lot of condensed milk, topped up with soda water from a siphon. The shakes were delicious and Percy and I thought we could undercut the market. For a few weeks our sales were phenomenal then Ma Weed complained to our Housemaster that we were ruining her business and we were closed down. On one occasion, in mid-production, a fag call went. I and all our customers immediately answered, but not Percy, who was too involved in his work. He paid the price later on his posterior.

After two weeks at the school one had to take the Fag's Test. Stephen Fry gives a good description of his experiences of this in his autobiography, Moab is My Washpot. He quotes the names of the twelve houses, which he had to recount and which he remembers well. There were thirteen in my day but Redgate closed in 1940. I can do better than Stephen and name each Housemaster of my time. The test gave me no problems as I have a retentive memory. I rolled off the names of the houses, the housemaster's, their nicknames, the geography and traditions of the school and also some public school slang such as 'tizzy' for sixpence and 'sassy' for cheeky.

In your first year you slept in a small dormitory of ten with one Polly. James Gavin was in charge of us and he was very kind, taking good care of us and checking that we were not homesick. In later life he went on the Everest Expedition of 1938 and became a Major General in the Army. He died aged 89 and I noticed his obituary in the paper.

After a year one moved to a big dormitory. This was T shaped and contained twenty nine beds; each one had its own cubicle with a washbasin, large jug of cold water and a chamber pot. There was a hook for your suit and just room for shirts and underwear to be hung up. Curtains could be pulled around the cubicle but you were only allowed to close them when dressing. Our beds were made by maids. One of the duties of a fag was 'time calling'. He had to wait for the Town's clock to chime seven and then call out, 'Seven o'clock, two past', to wake up the other 28 boys. The call was repeated at five past, ten past and by each minute up to seventeen past. The fag had to be two minutes ahead to coincide with the clock chiming at the quarter hour. Woe betide any fag who misjudged the strike. If boys were late it was a certain beating that evening. There were fifteen minutes to get to the Memorial Hall at the centre of Town by 7.30. It was a mad rush. There was no breakfast but cocoa downstairs which no one had time to drink. There was trouble if you did not make the Memorial Hall on time. There was an almighty rush at the two-door entrance when boys from the thirteen houses arrived at once. The school Polly's, who wore white boaters instead of the normal speckled ones, stood by the doors and closed them at the stroke of 7.30, but sometimes the crush was so great that they were pushed back. For those who did not make it Sergeant Major Bacovitch was waiting with his notebook. Once listed you had to parade in the quadrangle and march up and down for twenty minutes; this left only forty minutes to get to your house and back again for breakfast. After a quarter of an hour in the hall there was a three quarter hour lesson and then you rushed back to your house for breakfast and back for more lessons at 9.30.

I was seldom late but on the one occasion that I was we were paraded in front of Lorne House and, with no breakfast I felt faint. Backovitch could not have cared but the Housemaster of Lorne House, 'Bubbly' Hale came by and rescued me. In the classroom he had a reputation for ferocity but on this occasion he took me into his house and gave me coffee. I have never forgotten his kindness; I was never in his form but his action gave me a new view of humanity.

The water for washing was cold and we had so little time, so getting ready for school in the morning was a farce. As we got older the question of shaving arose. Most boys shaved in the evening in the changing rooms where there was hot water, or at weekends if they could get away with a 'once a week' shave. I remember Douglas Kendrew, my House Captain, came back for his last term with a large moustache. Had he trimmed it he might have got away with it, but the Headmaster disapproved and off it came. Few of the Masters were moustachioed. Three housemasters did have them, Shea, Hales and Smallwood; cleanshaveness was the order of the day. D.F. Walker, who was captain of the school and a fine cricketer, took great pride in his appearance and was reported to shave twice a day. He was later a master at Harrow and was killed in the war. There was a prize on Speech Day, given every third year, for the best captain of the school for the last three years. By coincidence the boy who was captain in the third year always won. Walker was not in the three year cycle so the Headmaster created a special prize for him. He went on to captain Oxford at cricket; I feel sure he would have played for England if he had not been killed in the war.

It was a great occasion when you had served your two years and were no longer a fag. At the end of it all there was a ritual. Standing on your bed in the dormitory you had to sing a song to the other 28 boys. I cannot sing a note and the nerves generated by the thought of this task spoilt my summer holidays. I was fourth in order to sing and listening to the others heightened my agony. Ernest English was ahead of me and he sang, appallingly, 'I am Sherlock Holmes, the Great Detective' I had to sing 'The Return of the Gay Caballero', a song made famous by the American balladeer Frank Crumit. It went as follows, -

> 'I am a Gay Caballero
>
> Coming from Rio Janero
>
> With nicely oily hair and full of hot air
>
> I am expert at shooting the billo'

Fortunately 'Gay' did not have its current meaning or my rendition would have caused a greater sensation than it did; the word we used was 'pansy'. I now have a CD of Frank's with the song on it.

Uppingham, like many Public Schools, had many traditions. I recall Rugby's first Head Girl recounting that she could drive sheep through the town and grow a beard. One of ours concerned the road from The Hall to the centre of the school. No one was allowed to walk on the right side unless they were from Constable's House. You were allowed to cross over to the newsagent's but had to return immediately. The tradition arose, obscurely, because Constable's was once located on that side of the road. Three sisters, known as Faith, Hope and Charity now lived in a house on that site.

Very few of the old shops have survived. The chemist is now a branch of Boots, but the cake shop, Binns and the outfitter Smalls are still there. On Sundays we wore tails instead of the black coats. There was a choice on the school's clothes list, tails or Eton jacket. I had an Eton jacket so my grandmother sent this off. At my first church service there was only one other boy so attired and I felt very juvenile. I quickly sent off a letter requesting tails. Grandmother would have prepared my father's trunk 29 years earlier. Perhaps this problem did not arise then.

Sunday afternoons were a horror. The idea in The Hall was that boys had to be occupied. Unless the weather was really bad we all had to be outside. Only the Top Table, those in their last year, had the option of staying in their studies or enjoying the housemaster's private garden. The Hall was rather isolated, being at one end of the Town so boys from other houses seldom came our way. If one wanted a walk there was just the village of Bisbrook, two miles away or a tramp over empty fields. Percy Kennedy and I often got into scrapes; once we were in a railway tunnel when a train came through. Although you were not meant to mix with boys from other years I often had company; on other occasions I was alone. I did not really like those lonely walks without even a dog for company. Once at a bottom of a hill I spied someone sitting at the top. It was Derek Gillespie and we joined up and walked back to the house together. On my return I was told off by the Polly's as he was two years younger than me and we should not have been together. Derek later became a good friend and we used to meet up on Old Boy's Days and have a drink. He was captain of cricket and gained a blue at Cambridge, later he qualified as a solicitor and died in 1981.

It is strange how one can vividly remember a day in one's life from a long time ago although there was not always particular reason to do so. I can visualise two such days at Uppingham in 1930, 80 years ago. It was a Sunday morning and we were trooping into Chapel when news spread that the Airship R101 had crashed. It was on its maiden voyage and the Aviation Expert Sefton Brancker and Lord Thompson, the Air Minister were on board, it claimed the lives of almost fifty passengers. The other occasion was my sixteenth birthday on 22nd March. We used to play cricket in the house quad and I was very keen on this. Often the seniors had the run of the quad and we had to wait until they had finished. On this day I was watching them when Anthony Heath saw me and said, 'Farmiloe is sixteen today. Let him join us'. The kindness of this action is embedded in my memory.

The toilets in the house were an ordeal. The cubicles had no doors and I found this lack of privacy embarrassing. There were some dilapidated toilets by the main school building, which did have doors, and I would patronise these. I am glad these barbarities have gone. In 2007 during a tour given by a girl pupil I was told the new studies have en-suite facilities.

Fortunately there was not much bullying in The Hall. It helped if you were a games player. However one victim was Henry Bulkeley, the son of an Old Uppinghamian. He was shy and not good at games and found things very difficult. I met up with him at one of the reunions in the 1950s. He was still rather shy and bookish and had found his niche as a prep school master.

Food at The Hall was not very plentiful and while lunch was substantial supper was just a snack. While in evening service we would leave tins of beans in hot water for eating on our return. Provisions were reinforced with allowances from home. A purchase required a signed chit from the housemaster. He never looked at the chits and one boy got a note for a pink elephant.

The boys were well-off and I expect this caused conflict in the town as it was the height of the depression and there was much poverty. But the school was vital to the local economy providing much employment. Tom Staples straddled this divide. He was about twenty years older than I and turned out to be a great friend. His wife was a cook in The Hall, which brought in a small income for their six children. Tom was a bookie's runner an occupation he kept until he died in the early 70s. Everyone in Uppingham knew Tom and he frequented all seven pubs. I gambled quite a lot and Tom placed all my bets. I used to buy The Daily Herald at Dalby's for the racing. This was frowned upon, not because of its sporting content, but because it supported Labour. Tom knew many Old Boys, placed bets for them, and would join them for drinks in the pubs. There is one story told by Tom about Percy Chapman, the English cricket captain. Tom went to Leicester to watch Percy play there for Kent and they had a drinking session during the lunch interval. When Percy was called to bat he told Tom he had had too much to drink and asked what to do. Tom told him to go in and hit everything. Percy may have been drunk but he hit a very fast sixty before he was out. Sadly in the end the drink got Percy.

I knew all of Tom's six children. The eldest son was in the army. Shirley, the eldest daughter, sadly died young. Next was Brenda, and a third daughter married a garage proprietor from Market Harborough. Sam was a brilliant cricketer and played for Uppingham Town and Malcolm was the youngest. I went to five Old Boy's Days before the war and five immediately afterwards and saw a lot of Tom. When I could afford it I stayed at The Falcon. Once a drinking friend of Tom's put me up and on another occasion Tom did. Mrs Staples provided a huge breakfast. That night there was a dance in the Village Hall, which was quite an experience with the Staples girls. Tom knew both my wives. In 1943 I was stationed at Leicester and Pat and I caught the bus over and we had some good times together. During the 50s and 60s Dorothy and I often stayed in Uppingham on our way north and we always had a drink with Tom. He and his pals used to hire a bus each year for an outing to London. I met up with them one year at the Elephant and Castle and was amazed by the amount of drink consumed. The Staples family lived at 11 The Quadrant, a row of council houses; later they moved to No. 9. They had a hard time in the 30s during the recession but after the war they prospered with successful businesses and marriages. Sadly now they have all moved away but Tom's name is often mentioned in the pubs.

Today, Speech Day and Old Boy's Day have been amalgamated but they used to be separate. Speech Day was for parents and the Old Boy's Day, which in fact lasted for two days, involved a two-day cricket match, concerts and receptions. Vera Brittain's Testament to Youth is well worth reading. She describes a Speech Day at Uppingham just before the first war. Her brother, Edward and his best friends, Roland Leighton and Victor Richardson were OUs and all were killed in the war. Roland was Vera's fiancé. She mentions the Musical Director, Sterndale Bennett, who was still there in my time.

Uppingham claims to be the first school where every pupil has their own study. This was not quite so for The Hall where there were 34 studies for 40 boys, the youngest shared. Thomas Belk was the under housemaster and he supervised the junior boys for prep in the Common Room. He was a much revered figure and lived all his life in the town. Dorothy and I used to visit him when we passed through, but he was not strict enough when he took prep and I shamelessly took advantage of him. I must say a word about Wignall, the excellent house handyman. He would do anything for the boys, was much liked, and was rewarded with hefty tips at the end of term.

Occasionally in the summer term there were outings when fleets of buses took us to places of interest. My favourite was the East of England Show at Peterborough. The school excelled at shooting and won the Ashburton Shield for public schools, but shooting was not my forte. Neither was swimming but every boy had to swim the length of the baths, a task I eventually accomplished. Music was done very well. Two celebrated Directors of Music covered eighty years between them, P.J.P David from 1865 to 1908 and Sterndale Bennett from 1908 to 1945. The latter's brother was more celebrated and wrote the song, Ten Green Bottles. There were many concerts in the Memorial Hall but I was not a lover of classical music and stoically sat on my hard bench waiting for the finale. Recently music has flourished at the school, which had produced members of the boy bands, Busted and McFly. I took music lessons from R.J.E.Oakley, who later became Musical Director at Bishops Stortford College. I did not take them seriously and played him up, but we struck up a friendship and in later days he came to my Mother's flat to play bridge. Today there is just one tune I can strum a few notes of Boys and Girls Come out to Play.

The Officers Training Corps played a large part in my life but I did not enjoy it and never rose higher than Private. It was voluntary but everyone felt obliged to join, except Derek Sleep, a kind of conscientious objector, but he joined the war in the RAF and graduated to a Flight Lt. At the end of the summer term there was a two week camp at Catterick or Strenshall but these were unpopular as no one wished to curtail their holiday. But in 1932 the house captain, John Gillespie, decided that the whole house should attend. I had already arranged to go to Royan in France and so escaped, but I was not popular. John was tragically killed at Tobruck in 1941.

Uppingham, with its sister school, Oakham, was founded in 1584. It made no great impact until the Old Etonian, the Revd Edward Thring was appointed Headmaster in 1853. He held this post until his death in 1887 and he transformed the school into one of the leading Public Schools of England. He became a national figure when, as a protest against inadequate drainage and an outbreak of typhoid in the Town, he moved the school for a year to Borth in Wales. During the absence the town, which relied economically on the school, modernised all the drains. During his Headmastership the school joined the Headmaster's Conference and he became its first Chairman. He also started the Headmistress's Conference and there is a photograph of him as the only male with all these august ladies. If a boy was late back from the holidays they were flogged. One father objected when his two sons, in their eighteenth & nineteenth year, missed the train back to school. He complained to the media, where Thring was classed as a cruel and sadistic Headmaster. I like the saying 'If Thring does not train his boys minds, he certainly teaches them to read their trains.

Celebrated OUs include Boris Karloff, born as William Pratt. Sir Malcolm Campbell and his son Donald Campbell, General Sir Brian Horrocks, who was Black Rod and who was much in demand in war documentaries.

I would like to say, without much relish, a word about homosexuality. Public Schools have a reputation for it, which is not surprising when a large number of 13 to 18 year-olds are cooped up. Bryan Mathews in his book 'By Gods Grace' describes how bad things were in my father's time. According to reports from old boys at the turn of the century, homosexuality was rampant. It was considered fashionable among some of the 'bloods' in the school to have attractive 'favourites' among the younger boys. It was probably better in my day; no doubt adolescents experimented but no lasting harm was done.

Today most public schools take girls, which must create a much healthier atmosphere. There were no girls anywhere near Uppingham in my day and we knew very little about them. Two exceptions were the attractive daughters of two masters, Erica Lloyd-Jones and Betty Bashford. I was told at a Speech Day recently that one boy dated Erica – quite an achievement. The Housemaster of West Deyne, P.B.King, came back at the start of one term with a 21 year-old wife; she turned quite a few heads. When I arrived at Uppingham I was in a state of blissful ignorance. My Prep School Headmaster's talk involving rabbits had left me no wiser. John Dickson was two years older than I and we were friends later on, he recounted, probably exaggerating, that, on a Saturday, night there was a queue outside one boy's study of boys seeking pleasure.

At The Hall you were confined to your study until after supper and only Polly's were allowed to move about. One had a liking for small boys and would make evening visits; Fred Tordoff was among this number. The Polly was found out, spared expulsion, and just demoted. The biggest scandal of my time involved maids; two boys were found romping around in one of their bedrooms. They were expelled and the Headmaster addressed us on the subject in disgust. This was probably inspired by snobbery rather than moral considerations. Another expulsion involved a boy stealing watches. I think he had mental problems and he should have been dealt with differently.

At Heath Mount my academic progress started slowly and then improved. I have an Uppingham school report from the summer term of 1930. Sadly history is not shown separately, but included in English, as this was my best subject (end of chapter). Those who were unlikely to make the sixth form were filtered into the Army and Engineering class, which was run by an OU, John Dain, who was sadly killed in the war. I went there and prospered. My house captain, Douglas Kendrew was similarly treated and demonstrated that this was no bar to later success. He captained England at Rugby, became a Major General, won the DSO with three bars and was Governor General of Western Australia.

A word about exams, I took my Common Entrance early and failed. This was a blessing in disguise as I was too young and I passed next time. The next exam I took was in 1933 and was the Preliminary for the Institute of Chartered Accountants, which I passed.

My last year was the most enjoyable. There were ten of us at the Top Table and we were granted privileges. We did not have to go for a walk on Sunday afternoons but could enjoy the housemaster's garden and its extensive walks, lawns and a tennis court. Also one boy was allowed a wind-up gramophone in his study. There was keen competition for this and I was luckily chosen.

For my first two years my housemaster was Major Shea, an elderly, easy-going man with a charming wife. She had a great personality, very bubbly and always talking. They had two daughters; Girlie was going out with a Pilot Officer Peacock who was stationed at nearby Wittering. We would spy on then canoodling in the driveway in the evening. The other daughter, Daphne was, just like her mother, very cheerful. She married P.F. Saunders who was a housemaster of Lorne House from 1931 until 1958, a long reign; the normal term is 15 years.

When Mrs Shea died the Major took rooms in Lorne House and I recall visiting him there when he was in his nineties. When Percy Chapman, later the English cricket captain, was the Uppingham captain, he met the visiting team from Rugby at the station and their captain was P.F. Saunders. He liked the school so much he became a master and married Daphne. After they retired they lived in a pleasant house in the town. Dorothy and I called on them once and Daphne reminded me how unhappy I was when I first arrived. In 1931 V.T. Saunders, (no relation), took over. His wife was a tall, and a quiet woman, quite different from Mrs Shea, but she was kind and I liked her. They had three children and I remember Cynthia, perhaps a couple of years younger than me, who married W.F. Shaw, a housemaster of Highfield and I enjoyed meeting up with her at a reunion in 2007. I shall be frank about V.T Saunders. I did not like him and he was not popular. His attitude was Victorian and he terrified the boys. He had a low opinion of me and felt that I could not assert authority. I resented that he did not appoint me a Polly. There should have been five out of a top table of ten, but he only picked three, cutting me out, and repeating the process for the next two terms as well.

Our relationship unsurprisingly did not improve after I had left when I, with some other Old Boys, took Cynthia drinking with Tom Staples to a Pub in Glaston and we did not return until 4 am. The Publican later committed suicide but these two events were not connected. I should add that I organised three Hall reunion dinners after the War and V.T. Saunders always came along. No doubt impressed by my organising abilities and my success in the world he told me that he had underestimated me at school. After that all was forgiven and I rather liked him.

I would like to say a word about some of my Uppingham friends. Dermot Milman was blessed with both sporting prowess and a fine brain, but the story that he absent-mindedly answered a Latin exam in Greek is apocryphal. He was in the cricket and rugby teams and represented England at rugby. He had a successful diplomatic career and inherited a baronetcy in 1962. Although not living in the area when I organised an East Anglican OU reunion at Henstead Hall, he gladly came along. Fred Tordoff was a great friend. He would visit me at both Hampstead and Henstead and I visited him at Baildon, near Shipley, in Yorkshire. He had shares in the men's outfitters shops I ran before the war and sadly we both lost money when the venture folded. I kept in touch with him all his life. Percy Kennedy and I were both fond of racing and we were fellow gamblers at Uppingham. In c. 1935 I was honoured to be his best man. He then lived in Ireland and worked as a flying instructor, keeping up flying to a great age. Although I kept in touch I did not see him for 70 years until a Speech Day in 2006, and the at The Hall reunion the next year. Percy and Renate, together with my daughter, Helen made up a good foursome but unfortunately was unable to make the 2010 Reunion.

I would like to say a word about the Masters. The one I recall above all others was T.B. Belk. He was the very epitome of Uppingham, first as a pupil, then as Head Boy, then at the age of 23 he became a master, a position he held for 37 years. On retirement he served as Librarian and lived in the Town in Leicester Road well into his eighties. Once at a cricket match, when he was a young master, my grandfather mistook him for a boy, embarrassingly asking him what he was going to do when he left. Looking young for ones age can be confusing. I remember when I was 33 and starting my accountancy practice a new client said I seemed too young to take on her financial affairs. On another occasion, staying at Horndean with Lady Brickwood I heard her remark to my mother, 'You would never think Douglas was seventeen. He looks far too young.' I am afraid I overheard and gave the good Lady a mouthful; I had a bad temper in those days.

To return to Belk, whenever Dorothy and I visited Uppingham we called in on him. He was confined to a chair and sat on the first floor of his house looking out of a window. He would call out an invitation to us to come up and always enquired after our hotel. The only time he ventured out was to the Sunday morning school service. He was looked after by D.G. Oswald, who lived next door and who joined the masters as a young man the year I left.

I can recall all the names of the housemasters and their Houses, J.C. Atkins at Highfield. The Revd 'Fergy' McNeile at Redgate, he delivered the most boring sermons, surprisingly as his brother was H.C. McNeil, alias Sapper, the author who wrote the Bulldog Drummond adventure books. E.W.C. Saunders Was at

Brooklands, he acted as Headmaster when R.H. Owen was in New Zealand for a year. 'Fatty' Gilkes, a pleasant man, was my first form master. His brother, A.N. Gilkes was much thinner, but never called 'Thinny', was housemaster of Meadhurst and later Highmaster of St.Paul's. Fatty became Headmaster of Dulwich. A.M. Smallwood, a former England Rugby International, was at The Lodge. He coached the team, which became almost unbeatable. The Revd C.C. Mountford was at West Bank. P.B.King, who had the young wife, was at West Deyne. H.St.J.B. Watson was at Brooklands. He had served as a captain in the war and suffered from shell shock. E.D. Ebden was at Constables. I was in his form and liked him but he had a sharp, sarcastic wit. He was a man of principal and one incident stands out. F.G.H. Chalk, a talented cricketer, who captained Kent and might have played for England if he had not been killed in the war, was due to go to Oxford for an exam. He held every school honour. To leave the school you needed a signed chit, but he forged Ebden's signature. On his return he was stripped of all his honours and reverted to being an ordinary boy for the rest of his last term. I may not know all the facts but I consider this punishment draconian.

Other Masters included F.W.Gilligan, an Essex County Cricketer and later a headmaster in New Zealand. C.C. Blagden was my form master. I remember him laying into the class saying we were a pampered lot and other boys of our age, (fifteen) had to go out to work to support their families. Vernon Kirwan was so disgusted by this rant that he stormed out. Blagden lived just opposite The Hall. One afternoon he came out of his house bleary-eyed. One wag observed that he must have been making love to his wife over the lunch break. We made a note to see if a baby arrived nine months later.

There was one master and a boy who must remain anonymous. The master was totally unsuited to his profession. He could have been a nice young man in the antique business, the type found in a Noel Coward play. The boy was tall, olive skinned and of good-looking Latin physique. Masters occasionally asked boys to tea, although I was never asked, and these two often had tea together. At the beginning of one term this master mysteriously did not return. In later life these two became an item.

Others on the staff who deserve a mention are Dawes, the school porter and Edwards, the cricket professional. Then there was Sergeant Major Bacovitch, the Gymnasium Instructor. In spite of his army rank he had no connection with the OTC. He was 5ft 3 inches of height, as broad as he was tall, with rippling muscles and a booming voice. All boys had to do two half-hour sessions a week in Baco's gym. He might have eighteen in hand with three times that number waiting in the gallery. The session was continuous exercise but if one boy slacked the whole of his line, about six, were sent up to the gallery to await another session. If you were unlucky half an hour could become three hours. When I returned on Old Boy's days I met Baco again and he was entirely a different person – very polite and humble. No doubt Sandhurst Sergeant Majors are the same – treating their Cadets like vermin but when they are Officers they call them 'Sir'. Baco had a daughter who was pretty and the living image of her father.

I always remember a story on snobbery I heard at school. The captains of the various games used to arrange whom they played in the year. One school wrote to Eton for a fixture against them. The Eton captain wrote back 'Harrow we play, Winchester we have heard of, but who are you?'

My father was at Uppingham with Thring's successor. One old boy, who later became a well-known painter hated it there and said "I was kicked, hounded, caned, flogged and hair brushed morning noon and night"

Now a word about the staff at The Hall, the maids we saw but never spoke to, the kitchen staff we did not even see. It was not until a much later date that I found out that Mrs Staples was the cook. There Mrs Woodcock was the matron. I was most fortunate in the two matrons I came across in my school career and received much kindness from both of them. The one at Heath Mount was a relative of the Old Marlbrarian Headmaster, the Revd Wells and was treated on par with the Masters. At Uppingham Mrs Woodcock was a rung lower on the pecking order. She made life bearable in my early years. Her relatives kept a shop in the High Street called Woodcock's and when my son Jay was born in nearby Birstall, Leicestershire, Mrs Woodcock's sister was midwife.

Finally a word about the Headmaster, the strict, aloof, fearsome, Revd Reginald Herbert Owen, he was known as 'The Man.' In many ways he was a remarkable person and his discipline was formidable. Once at a cricket match a boy swore for which he received a beating, in spite of being in the Second XV. 15 stone and nearly 6 foot. Owen hated publicity and was much displeased about press reports of a boy's motor bike riding achievements in the holidays. My grandfather had to forewarn him that my name would appear in the paper in an anniversary announcement of my father's death, which added that I was to follow him to his old school. He was a good fund-raiser. In those days the house masters often owned their boarding houses. This was unsatisfactory and some cut back on food to make money for themselves. He persuaded the governors to buy them out.

On the first morning of term the new boys paraded in the Assembly Hall. In the winter term there could be one hundred. Each boy called out his name to Owen and he would look at the boy and return the call. If he made a mistake he would start the process again at the beginning. If he spoke to a boy during his walks he would always remember his name. This was an achievement as one year there could be six Smiths, the following one three could have left and three more arrived so Smith Sextus would now become Smith Minimus.

He taught Latin to the Sixth Form and had plenty to do with the Polly's but did not cross paths much with a humble boy like me. In later life, when in the Army, I wrote to him and received a nice reply. His grip extended to the masters and their wives. If any of these were lax in their appearance or smoked in the wrong place he would write a note reprimanding them. I have a high opinion of him but he was rather less than human. One might imagine that he was at least middle aged but in fact in 1928 he was only 33, having been appointed five years earlier at the age of 28, the youngest Head Master of that time.

Uppingham Sport

For the benefit of my Uppingham readers I have noted down some memories of sport in my time. I have already described how, due to an unsatisfactory cricket test in my first season, I was confined to five years of playing in League and House matches for The Hall. My collection of Hall magazines recording the scores is incomplete but I can set out the records I do have. In my first season we won the first round against Redgate by four wickets thanks to the brilliant cricketer, John Gillespie. In the next round we were against Constables; we made 176 in the first innings of which Gillespie contributed 114 and they were all out for 143. For the second innings they made only 55 with Gillespie's bowling figures being 7 wickets for 25 runs, so we only had to score 33 to win. But Gillespie was quickly out and our batting collapsed and 7 wickets had gone before we reached the 33. The magazine recorded, 'Farmiloe is especially to be congratulated on his innings'. I do not know my score but I must have helped quite a bit. In the next round we were overwhelmed by Medhurst who won by an innings and 72 runs. In the league for that year I had some useful innings and bowled a bit. Only once did I score more than fifty. At evening supper one called out to the Housemaster your league score and V.T.Saunders would note this down and keep averages. Those who made over fifty, and this was infrequent, were applauded.

1930 was the next season and I was still in the Under 16s, but without Gillespie we were a weak side. The following season, disappointingly, I did not make the team and often ended up as 12th Man. The final against Medhurst saw high scores but we ran out of time and the result was a draw. Gillespie, our captain, just missed his century and Fred Tordoff made 71. Their Captain was D.F.Walker, who later captained Oxford. Tragically both captains were killed in the war.

In 1928 on the Rugby field we won the Over 16 House Cup, beating Farleigh by 22 to 0. D.A Kendrew, who a year later was playing for England was in our team, but on the other hand E.B. Pope, also later an England International who was born in 1911, was on the other side. Winning a place in the house rugby team was not difficult as fifteen players had to be found from a pool of forty boys. I enjoyed my Rugby and, being too light for the scrum, played as a three-quarter. In 1929 our Under16 team was thrashed 67-0 by School House. Percy Kennedy was Full Back and I on the wing where I doubt the ball very often reached me.

In my last Spring term I played some enjoyable Hockey but I never achieved the heights gained by my Father who was in international trials. Fives suited me, as it was an individual game. We had our own Fives court at The Hall so practising was easy. The game is like squash except you use a gloved hand to strike the ball; we played the Eton version where there was a box against the wall, which you played off. Fred Tordoff was a good player and was in the School Four and played in the Inter-schools tournament in the holidays. He stayed with me at Avening House for the fixture but the letter telling him the time when he was playing arrived late and he missed his match. Tennis was not a serious sport but we had a court at The Hall and I played in my last term. I am glad to see that it is now a major sport. Soccer, sadly, was never played.

I remember in 1931, when I was sixteen J.C.G. Grieve and D.L.K Milman were chosen to play in the English Under 19 Rugby XV. They were new to London and I suggested they lunched at my grandmother's house. Chambers met them at the station and it was a feather in my cap to entertain such important sportsmen. Grieve was sadly killed on active service in 1942. He suffered from Alopecia, which meant he was completely bald but this did not bother him at all. I remember Mrs Shea telling me that when he arrived at the school she and Mr Shea had no forewarning of this condition from his parents and it was a bit of a surprise. He was over 6ft tall and a formidable Rugger player on the wing; nobody could catch him. His younger brother arrived four years after me and was quite short and had plenty of hair. He came to stay at Henstead Hall with his family for a week one summer when Dorothy and I were running it as a hotel and we had plenty to talk about. He died in 1990.

Now a word about the inter-school Rugger matches. The one against Rugby was a local derby and in my time the scores were 5-6, 11-11, 0-3, 23-3 and 3-3. We won two of the three fixtures against Haileybury, four out of the five against Tonbridge and both matches against Oundle. The scores against other teams were, RAF Cranwell 40-0 to us, Brasenose College, Oxford 22-0 to us and again to us University College Oxford, 20-5. Our rugby field was called The Leicester and after each match there was a bit of a ritual. The spectators would crowd around the pavilion and the teams, except the captain, retire to the dressing room. Then, if anyone was to be awarded his colours, that player would return to the field and the captain would pass a ribbon around his middle, thus awarding him his 1st XV Cap.

Today for safety reasons I gather that due to the physical side of playing rugby that no school matches can involve boys playing this game if there is more than a two year gap between ages.

However in my day there were no such rules and many of the matches were between boys and men. The boys of Uppingham were expected to win against older players and invariably did. I cannot recall any injuries during those matches and I think there were three main reasons why the Uppingham boys won their games.

1. A better coaching system as after all the coach was an International.

2. A keener desire to win.

3. Perhaps the most important. They were usually much fitter than their opponents.

In my time there were two exceptional cricketers, F.R.G. Chalk and D.F. Walker who both later captained Oxford. They both later would have played for England, I feel, if they had not been killed in the war. Here are the results of the inter-school Cricket matches –

Repton Won 2, Lost 1, Drawn 1. (One win by an innings of 122 runs).

Shrewsbury Won 2, Lost 0, Drawn 1. (One win by an innings of 152 runs).

Haileybury Won 2, Lost 0. Drawn 2. (As with the Rugby matches the games were very close).

Oundle Won 3, Lost 0, Drawn 0.

Nine wins and one loss is a very good record. The captain of each team would administrate the game and he would post notices on the board in the Colonnade. The other teams we played were the Notts Amateurs, the Leicester Gentlemen and the Free Foresters. The latter fielded a strong team of mainly County cricketers including the fast bowler G.O. (Gubby) Allen. His average was 6 for 36 and we were bowled out for 145, with D.F. Walker scoring a duck and the Foresters replying with 150 for one wicket.

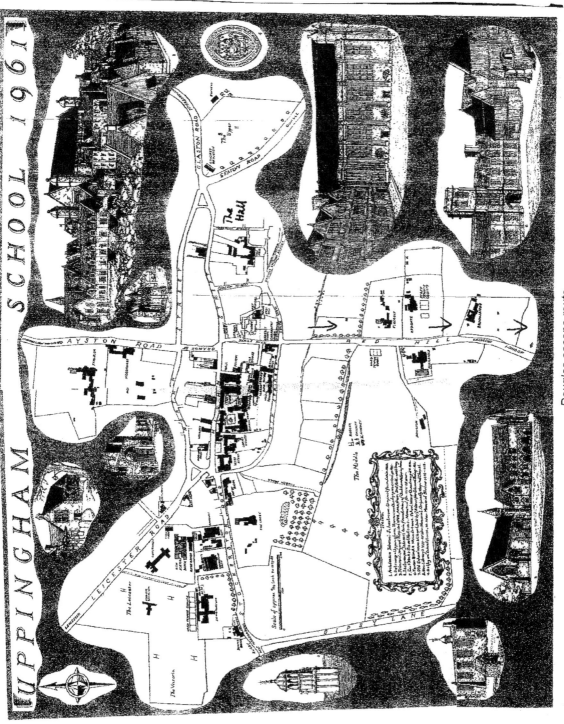

Douglas escape route

UPPINGHAM SCHOOL.

TERM II, 1930.   Form...... L IV a

Term's Report of the Progress and Conduct of _____ Farmiloe

DIVINITY.	Fair KA
LATIN AND GREEK.	Considerable improvement since half-term. Has worked well and is making good progress KA
FRENCH.	He needed pressure to get him to work but he has done definitely better of late. B.H.L.
GERMAN.	
ENGLISH SUBJECTS. ESSAY.	Weak in expression and arrangement. However he is trying hard and is improving KA
NATURAL SCIENCE.	Quite satisfactory work & progress CCH
MATHEMATICS.	At last he is beginning to settle down to work carefully. A great improvement! JRC.
MUSIC.	Rather slow, but nevertheless has improved greatly this term. Must work hard R.G.E.O.
DRAWING.	He has worked well and is learning HSR.
GENERAL CONDUCT.	Conduct very good. I am glad to see there is an all round improvement in his work. RVShea

He is low in the School and must determine to move more rapidly. He has begun to try.

R. H. Owen.   *Headmaster.*

Corps Promotions :—To Corporal : McIver. To Lance-Corporal : Welch, Milman, and Thompson.

We congratulate D. A. Kendrew on getting his England cap, and on going on the Rugby Union Tour to New Zealand.

The following new boys came this term :—E. W. Aman and H. J. L. Bulkeley.

VALE.

W. G. Foster. Came January, 1926; M.M.V.b.; House Praepostor, September, 1929 : 2nd XV., 1928-29.

FAGGING.

A Polly, in his study quiet,
Hears outside an awful riot.
He mutters to himself, "My hat!
I'll give them something to laugh at!"

And so the fag, all sad with gloom,
Is summoned to the changing room,
And there he sees his awful doom,
And wonders what will be his tomb.

For of escape there is no trace,
And so the ceremony takes place,
Towards the victim they take their pace,
And out he walks with a different face.

Fagging is an awful bore,
With Pollies there is always war.
In two terms time there'll be no more,
And to all calls I'll shut my door.

ONE OF THEM.

CRICKET.

UNDER XVI. HOUSE MATCHES.

FIRST ROUND.—THE HALL v. HIGHFIELD.

Having won the toss we batted and made only 23, of which Farmiloe made 9. The bowling of Christopherson and Carr seemed too strong for them. Highfield then went in and made a total of 101, McCosh making 24. Battersby bowled particularly well and finished with the excellent analysis of 7 for 24. The fielding of the side was very good indeed, Watkinson holding a particularly good catch in the slips. Tordoff mi. also kept wicket very well.

We then batted again and made 69. Farmiloe again was the only batsman to offer any resistance, collecting in all a patient 18. Welch mi. and Langley put up quite a bright last wicket stand.

SCORES:—

THE HALL.

	FIRST INNINGS.			SECOND INNINGS.	
Carter, b. Horsfall		2	b. Carr ma.		0
Farmiloe, b. Clive		9	b. Clive		18
Robinson, b. Clive		2	b. Horsfall		2
Battersby, c. McCosh mi., b. Christopherson		0	b. Horsfall		2
Watkinson, c. McCosh ma., b. Christopherson		0	c. Horsfall, b. Carr ma.		0
Tordoff mi., b. Carr ma.		2	b. Clive		8
Aman, not out		2	b. Carr ma.		7
Bulkeley, c. McCosh mi., b. Carr ma.		0	c. Carr ma., b. Sinclair...		4
Kennedy, c. McCosh ma., b. Carr ma.		0	l.b.w. b. Sinclair		0
Welch mi., c. Sinclair mi., b. Christopherson		1	b. Sinclair		13
Langley, run out		0	not out		6
Extras		5	Extras		9
Total 23			Total 69		

Copy of Hall magazine 1930, showing under XVI House Match, opposite a poem on 'fagging'

CHAPTER FIVE

1933-1936

It was mid July and I was walking up Uppingham High Street, my eighteenth birthday was four months behind me and darkness was setting in. I looked to the sky, my mind was buzzing away, for by this time tomorrow I would have my freedom, something I had been eagerly anticipating for five years; no more discipline, freedom to wear what I liked, freedom to do what I liked. I was on my way, with all the other leavers, to the Memorial Hall for a farewell lecture from the headmaster the subject, our journey into the big wide world. Usually we were not allowed out after dark, the exceptions being a parental visit or three hours of The Messiah on hard benches. There were no celebrations for our last night at school. We had had too much discipline installed and the idea of going mad did not occur. 'Teenagers' had not been invented. I did not enter that phase until I was twenty-one and had money, then for three years I was out of control. Then we thought we were untouchable and had no fear of the consequences; pranks were the order of the day and we had not a care in the world. There was a comment in the papers that the war babies were now twenty-one and there was speculation as to how we would turn out. Well this is how; it was the fashion to steal all the ash trays from the best hotels and I had a good collection. Neville Southwell outdid me, specializing in coloured lights from Belisha Beacons. Interestingly the working class bypassed all this activity. They had no money and were keen to get what jobs or apprenticeships that were going. Once they found a job they expected to stay there for the rest of their working lives.

My dream of dressing how I liked soon evaporated. At school it was dark striped trousers, dark coat, white shirt, stiff collar and boater. Convention dictated that for the next thirty years there was no change, except a bowler replaced a boater. In the fifties, when Anthony Eden wore a homburg there was some relief. Matters got worse when, during my years in the army, I had to wear a khaki suit and no tie. But at least now I had pockets in my trousers, at Uppingham these were stitched up, as having hands in pockets was considered slovenly. Indeed pockets were not unstitched until the seventies. One advantage of the Uppingham discipline is that I never got into the habit of swearing. I might occasionally use words like damn and hell but never the F word or similar.

In the thirties Uppingham had a railway station and at the end of term there were two trains, one going north, the other south, to take us home. We were all relieved to put our civilian clothes on after three months. Packets of cigarettes appeared from nowhere. Nobody thought of smoking during the term. I recall one boy needed a cigarette as a prop for his part in a house play. He made the mistake of lighting it and received six of the best. One of my friends, Pemberton Robinson, who lived in County Durham, joined me for the day. Pemberton later became a Solicitor and died in 1991. His son followed him to Uppingham and now lives in France. At Euston, Chambers, the chauffeur met us with the Double Daimler complete with the Farmiloe crest painted on the door. I had two pieces of luggage, a huge trunk and a tuck box, which at the beginning of term was crammed full of food, but this only lasted a few weeks and was now empty. Pemberton and I saw a film in the West End. Films in those days started in the West End and only nine months later moved to the provinces.

I was not to start work as an Articled Clerk with a firm of Chartered Accountants until the spring of the next year and grandmother had now left Avening House for Henstead Hall, so I spent the next eight months living at Oakley Court Cottage, whose name was a slight misnomer as it was a large sprawling bungalow with five bedrooms, and about five acres of grounds and a lawn leading down to the Thames. It had its own mooring, a motor launch and a boat for rowing and punting. At the front of the house was another lawn surrounded with trees and it shared a half mile drive with the big house, Oakley Court. We were placed midway between Maidenhead and Windsor and were in the fashionable village of Bray, whose centre was about two miles away by either road or river. Not the famous Bray, a village in Ireland whose vicar became known for his oscillating allegiances, but another one, which was exclusive and contained many pretty, old-looking cottages. Uncle Shirley, my mother's brother, rented the cottage for three years from 1932, my mother, Dodie, lived there as well and I spent much of my summer holidays there in my late teens. Shirley George Kingsley was born about 1893 and educated at Framlingham College. As a young man he emigrated to the Argentine and pioneered aerial photography and commercial aviation. He returned to England at the outbreak of World War One and served with 14 Squadron, Royal Flying Corps when he won the MC. The citation stated, 'He was attacked by three hostile machines and shot down. To ensure that his machine would be destroyed, he deliberately landed in the sea at great risk to himself, as he had been wounded and only with difficulty swam ashore.' After the war he returned to the Argentine enlarging his fortune. He came back to the UK in 1931 and lived a comfortable life from his accumulated wealth. Later he entered the hotel and restaurant business owning a chain called the De Hems group; properties included The Comedy Restaurant in the West End and the Alexandra Hotel in Hastings. In the First War the RAF maintained

Army ranks so between the wars he retained the rank of Major, equivalent to Squadron Leader. On the outbreak of World War II he rejoined the RAF as a desk-bound Wing Commander. Strangely after that war he abandoned his higher service rank and reverted to Mr Kingsley. In his personal life he was extremely selfish. He had married Lois during World War One and David was born in 1917. A daughter was born just after the war and she was considered an encumbrance, interfering with Shirley's career in the Argentine and Lois's pursuit of pleasure. While Shirley was in South America Lois was in the South of France and David was left in England. This daughter was adopted, only to turn up fifty years later on David's doorstep to say, 'I'm your sister.' None of my generation knew of her existence. David spent the summer holidays in the south of France with his mother and from about the age of nine was put on a train to return to the UK under the care of a guard, an activity he became quite used to. Shirley and Lois met up again for a while in 1923 for a holiday in England and the consequence was another daughter, Diana. She was farmed off somewhere in the Midlands only to reappear eight years later at Oakley Court Cottage; a terrifying experience for her to acquire all those relations at once. David was the nearest I ever had to a brother. His nickname was 'Buster'; Buster Keaton being in vogue at the time, but when Shirley returned this name was banned.

The other family in the cottage were the Hindes, who consisted of Kerry, the mother, and daughters, Mary and Ginka, aged 15 and 5 respectively. Kerry was vivacious and red-haired and you could not help getting on well with her, she was good friends with Dodie and Shirley and indeed with everybody. The Hindes arrived from the Argentine at the cottage in 1935 and stayed for about a year. Kerry's catch phrase was, 'I'll be seeing yah,' a corruption of Abyssinia, which was on everybody's mind after Mussolini's invasion. Shirley had been very friendly with them in Buenos Aires and the husband Norman never came to England. There was a question mark over Shirley's relationship with Kerry. He was a lady's man and, as David said, 'Too fond of women.' David walked out with Mary, who was a tall, attractive blond who liked a stroll in the evening. There was speculation as to how romantic these strolls were. When David was away I took his place when everything was very innocent. Mary made a return visit in 1935 and by this time she was a very striking young woman. I would see her quite often and after the war we met up again; she was the nearest I ever had to a sister. I often played with little Ginka when she was five. She was an adorable child, bilingual in English and Spanish, her hair arranged in curls and full of energy. Had she gone into films she could have rivalled Shirley Temple. She demanded that I play with her all the time, which I quite happily did; I was forever giving her piggy backs or charging around the lawn. Alas on a visit to England three years later she had become quite serious-minded and the sparkle had gone.

The big event of that summer was the making of a film at the end of our drive. It was called Wild Boy and featured the most famous greyhound of the day, Mick the Miller. David and I would go down most days hoping to be enlisted as extras, but we had no luck. More successful was Shirley's cook, Mrs Wellbeloved who got a walk-on part. Little was David to know that one day he would be deputy chairman of British Lion Films. The nearest I ever got to stardom was to be interviewed a few years ago in the village pub by Radio Suffolk. I had prepared something on my experiences on the County and District Councils but my interviewer was only interested in my memories of the Southwold Branch Railway Line that closed in 1929. Mick the greyhound, when he died, was not allowed to rest quietly in a grave. He was stuffed and is there for all to see at the National History Museum's branch at Tring.

The only shadow of that summer was Emma, not another young lady who liked evening strolls, but the novel by Jane Austin. I had to read it and write an essay for school on it and I kept procrastinating. Since then Jane Austin has been one of my favourite authors, but I find Emma the least interesting of her books.

The cottage was a house where many guests came and went and as I was not too busy I would go up to London on occasions for the day. Once Uncle Shirley took me up and arranged to pick me up at Crockford's, the bridge club, for the return journey. Come midnight he was not there so I phoned up to find out that he had forgotten me and was in bed. He was not best pleased to have to drive for two hours to rescue me.

It was at Oakley Court Cottage that romance first entered my life. She was called Moira and lived in a charming cottage in Bray. Moira was sixteen, slightly buxom and with the prettiest face I had ever seen. She lived in one of the charming Bray cottages with her mother, who had a limp following an accident. When young she must have been most attractive as she had been a girlfriend of Jack Buchanan (the famous actor). In a way I fell in love with Moira. I took her by bus to the pictures in Maidenhead and Uncle Shirley picked us up. His car was full and so Moira sat on my lap – a thrilling experience I have not forgotten. We saw a lot of each other but when I moved to London the visits faded out. But we must have kept in touch, as she was involved in the only motor accident I had when someone was hurt. I was in my Jaguar visiting her brother in Hampshire. A motorcyclist, going too fast, swerved to avoid us and landed in the ditch. We looked after him while waiting for the ambulance, but I do not think he was too badly hurt, as we never heard any more from the authorities. I shall never forget my first date or the girl with the smiling face.

When I started my articles in London I found rooms with Mrs Clifford at 32

Buckland Crescent, Swiss Cottage. These were rooms, and not digs, which I was to experience in the war; digs are different in that all the tenants eat together. I had read my history and in olden times gentlemen came to London and took rooms. Sherlock Holmes had rooms in Baker Street. I felt very grand and grown up in my new accommodation, which consisted of a large sitting room, bedroom, bathroom and WC. There was no kitchen but there was a point to make tea. A maid brought up breakfast every morning and later she cleaned the rooms, otherwise I had to eat out, except on Sunday when Mrs Clifford served a lunch. While at Mrs Clifford's I purchased a wind-up gramophone and started a large collection of 78 rpm records. My first two records were Night and Day and a Lew Stone tune, The Buggy Song, a catchy item about a cowboy, which I still play today. I started work in March 1934, the month of my nineteenth birthday, with Jocelyn, Miles, Page and Co, Chartered Accountants of 28 King Street in the City of London. The offices were in the heart of the city, off Cheapside, and close to the Bank and Moorgate. We had a good view of the Guildhall and could see the comings and goings of the Lord Mayor. No 28 was a tall, narrow building with four floors and a basement. The accommodation may have been satisfactory once, but the business had outgrown the space and the corridors were packed with files, so moving from room to room was difficult. The firm was among the top five in the UK, Jocelyn was no longer there when I arrived and Miles was eighty. He came to the office most days but I do not know how much work he did. Page was another elderly gentleman and only appeared on rare occasions, but still drew a substantial salary. In the end he was pushed out. The remaining partners were reasonably young and active.

Each partner was allowed two articled clerks, a profitable matter as my grandmother had to pay a £300 premium for me, about £14,500 in today's money. We received no wages, just a Christmas bonus. At my first Christmas we were paraded in front of the partners and the bonuses were distributed. Mine was a £10 note. Old Miles asked whom I was articled to and I replied, to his surprise, 'You Sir', Algernon Osmond Miles used to go on cruises with my great aunt Popsy in the previous century, which is why I was articled to him; he had been President of the Institute back in 1910.

Although I was a new boy we were not treated like office boys, making the tea etc; being unpaid we were similar to midshipmen in the Navy. To take the service analogy further the Partners were the colonels and majors while the articled clerks were the junior officers; the rest of the staff, of which there were plenty, were the other ranks. Whenever work was short we were sent round to the Chartered Accountants Hall in Moorgate, supposedly to study for our exams. The pecking order amongst the articled clerks was like school. To start with I was treated patronisingly, like a fag. The two senior article clerks, who were both about 24 and very debonair, were from aristocratic families. They names were Henderson and Mount. I was pleased then when new clerks arrived who were junior to me and I made a number of new friends. The first to arrive was Donald Urry who later became a director of Debenhams. Others were Peter Cox who had a very sweet girlfriend who took a fancy to me. Then there was Davis of 48 Bowrons Avenue, Wembley whom I have a letter from when he joined the Army. Finally my cousin David Kingsley joined. He put his training to good use becoming a successful Finance Director of Boulting Brothers.

We were not meant to mix socially with the 'other ranks' but I had always wanted to play soccer. Rugby was played at Heath Mount, although Captain Morgan, the master-in-charge, introduced soccer just before I left, and Uppingham was exclusively a rugger school. Jocelyn's had a soccer team that played on a Saturday afternoon run by Mr Peacock, one of the staff. I could not resist it and joined, much to the disapproval of the other articled clerks.

Our dress code was rigid; bowler hat, gloves carried but never worn and umbrella, never unfolded even if it was raining. Our biggest client was Debenham's. It was a huge undertaking and included Marshall and Snellgrove, many of the provincial shops in the North, the Bobbie's chain on the South Coast and the exclusive Caley's at Windsor. Other clients were Brown Brothers, the motor and aero part traders, and Eveready. There were no calculators and one could spend days casting stock sheets; casting being the technical name for adding up. This became so automatic that you could think of other things at the same time and still spot an error. Another tedious job was checking postings from one ledger to another – the senior clerk would call out the figures to the junior one.

Every summer an articled clerk would go with a senior to Leeds for six weeks to audit Marshall's departmental store. We would travel up by train, which had a cinema. I went up with a chap called Hill. He was a bit pompous but easy to get on with. His family were connected with Hanbury's who made the marvellous blackcurrant lozenges sold in tins. Later we were joined by McGubbin, a very pleasant man approaching sixty, with a walrus moustache. He told me the advantage of age was that one always had respect. We stayed at the best hotel, The Metropole, and received a guinea a day for expenses and outside meals – all charged to Debenham's. The tradition was that the articled clerks took out the good-looking Marshal's lift girl. I followed this tradition and we had some pleasant meals at Hagenbach's, and Hill and McGubbin did not see too much of me. Consolidating all the Debenham's accounts at the year-end was a formidable task dreaded by the Partners. Fortunately this was left to Mr Hunt, who was not qualified, but had been there so long he knew everything.

I resigned my articles in May 1936; just after I had turned twenty one and just before I was due to sit the Intermediate Exam. This rash action was inspired by the call to freedom and by the fact that I now had some money. It was foolish and I have always regretted it. After the War I was allowed a two year exemption and recommenced for nine months, this time with no premium to pay. In fact in the 1950s I could have taken the exam any time but the Authorised Public Accountants, to whom I was attached in the eighties, were accepted by the Board of Trade so I did not. My grandmother was pleased to get half her premium back and no doubt there was another articled clerk with £300 to take my place.

But to return to romance Topsy was my next girlfriend. She was opposite to Moira in both size and class, being a sleek and lovely girl of eighteen. I do not recall where we met but she had come from Wales to work as an assistant sales lady at Benthall's Departmental Store in Kingston. While I was always in awe of Moira I am afraid I always took advantage of Topsy. I suspect she looked up to me, but matters must have been quite serious as I recall travelling by train to Abergavenny to meet her parents, but in the end things faded away.

Two families I had much to do with were the Booths and the Killars. Both wives were widowed by the time I knew them and each family had three children who were all educated privately, and both, since the death of the breadwinner, lived in reduced circumstances. Roy Booth was my contemporary at Heath Mount and he went on to Highgate. He had an attractive sister called Molly whom Peter Ginsberg, another Heath Mount friend, much admired. The Booths lived on a select estate in Highgate village. The estate was like a park with tennis courts where, no doubt, Roy learnt his tennis. He later coached at the Paddington Sports Club and at Frinton-on-Sea. I would go to the club at Paddington with Roy to play tennis and have a few drinks. I recall meeting Charlie Coburn there, then in his eighties, who made his name with the song, The Man who Broke the Bank in Monte Carlo'. Roy had two friends who made up a foursome; one was Spanish and, having a car, led the way. The other was Tim Killar, who was rather stout, very good natured and often absentminded. Once his mother asked him to take the dustbin out for collection and, forgetting to leave it by the front door, he walked up the road with it.

The four of us once went for a week to a holiday camp in the south of England. It was not an enjoyable experience and I am afraid I learnt to indulge in now what is called 'binge drinking'. One of Tim Killar's older sisters, Margaret, caught my eye. She was 29 or 30 and this was the only time I was ever entangled with an older woman. She was dark-haired, attractive, wore large ear-rings in the gypsy style. We got on well and I recall she was liberal with her affections. My mother knew the family well and I took her down to Oakley Court Cottage for a weekend. The families would have been agreeable to a marriage but I am sure my mother was relieved when it did not happen. She would not have approved of her unsophisticated son marrying a woman of the world. However I was very fond of her and the age difference never occurred to me.

My twenty first birthday party was held at The Mayfair Hotel and I invited about twenty friends. These were mainly from Heath Mount also my cousin David Kingsley and Fred Tordoff. My grandmother kindly paid for a private room and we had dinner and drinks, somebody suggested we should go to a nightclub afterwards. This was Aliki's and my introduction to our way of life and from then on we were inseparable. But, I am ashamed, even to this day, that I did not invite Tim and Margaret. The reason being that there was a new love in my life, Aliki, and I did not want the two to meet. Margaret later married a Canadian and soon after died after a minor operation to her toe. So tragic as she deserved to get so much out of life. The Killars continued to welcome me and I recall spending much of the first Christmas after the war with them.

The Sleap family also played a large part in my life at this time. Derek Touchet Sleap was a few months older than I but arrived at The Hall two terms after me so was my junior. We were not friends at school where I found him aloof and morose. He hated games and was in the school choir so our interests did not overlap. As I mentioned earlier he was the only boy not to join the OTC, but he did get a Commission in the RAF during the war. After Uppingham I somehow got to know his mother and I saw a great deal of her and her fifteen-year-old daughter, June. The whole family were very short sighted and wore pebble glasses. Like Mrs Booth and Mrs Killar she was a widow but the family were well-off and lived in a luxurious flat in Albert Hall Mansions overlooking Hyde Park. Mrs Sleap was a bundle of fun and I got on really well with both mother and daughter. June was just like her mother and she and I had a brother-sister relationship. Once June took a liking to a member of the Crazy Gang, Knox of the duo, Nervo and Knox. On one occasion we managed to get through to Knox in his dressing room on the telephone. June's alluring voice charmed dear Knox who wished to ask her out. Little did he know that he was talking to a fifteen-year-old school-girl.

Has one ever seen a pretty girl and thought, 'If only we could meet she would be just the girl for me.' Just a passing dream of what might have been! Anyway on the night of King George's Silver Jubilee in 1935 Mrs Sleap, June and I (Derek, as usual was not there) were in the crowds in Piccadilly just by Eros. A car came round, crawling in the heavy traffic, with a most attractive blond hanging out of the window. She caught my eye and gave me a kiss. Ten minutes later she came by again and there was another kiss. Twice more this happened but there was no kiss number five. What might have come from all this? That evening often crops up in my thoughts.

I was also in Piccadilly for VE and VJ days and for George VI's funeral, one of Uncle Shirley's hotels was on the route and I had a good view of the procession. The slow march of all the Sovereigns, Presidents and Prime Ministers was an impressive sight. But I missed George V's lying-in-state when Uncle Shirley had a preview before the public were allowed in and witnessed the late Monarch's four sons standing guard over the coffin. I vividly recall Edward VIII's abdication. I felt very strongly about the way he was pushed out and blamed the Establishment and the Church. On the day of the actual abdication there was talk in the papers about raising an Army for the defence of the King. I phoned Fred Tordoff and we agreed to join but the call to arms came too late.

Sport has been one of my passions and I must chronicle my involvement. The fame of yesterday's sporting heroes has necessarily faded but their names and achievements are worth bringing into the limelight again. Let us start with Rugby. I followed the English Rugby team with interest as it was captained by my old head of house, D.A. Kendrew and I was lucky to be at Twickenham when the most spectacular try ever was made. Prince Alexander Obolensky, at the 1936 match when England played New Zealand, ran three quarters of the length of the field outwitting the entire opposition. This was the first time England had beaten the All Blacks and that evening they went to The Metropole Hotel in Northumberland Avenue to celebrate only to find that their opposition was staying there.

When I was very young cricket was my greatest love. My favourite player was the Irishman, Patsy Hendren of Middlesex and England. Once my grandfather introduced him to me at Lords and for two Easter holidays grandfather paid for me to have coaching there. It was with considerable excitement that I changed in the rooms in the Pavilion and then went out through the Long Room. One of my batting tutors was Jim Smith, the Middlesex fast bowler. He was a hopeless bat, going in last for his county. I do not know how he was able to teach batting, having such lack of talent in that department; if by any chance his bat did connect with the ball, he was so powerful that it was a six. I was eleven in 1926 when I first saw the Australians at Lords and it seems only yesterday. I also saw the great Australian touring teams of 1930 and 1934 when McCabe and the elegant Kippax were the stars, together with the complimentary pair of spinners, Mailey and Grimmett. These names may not connect with my readers but that of Don Bradman will. I first saw him in 1934 and without doubt there will not be another batsman like him. It was like watching a machine. When he played his last match at Lords the passionate cheering unnerved him and he was out for a duck. Up until then his average was over a century but the duck reduced it to 99.7 runs per innings.

I was lucky enough to be present at another interesting moment in cricket history; the MCC were playing at Lords. They had ten amateurs in their team and just one professional, Patsy Hendren. Percy Chapman led the amateurs out of the Lords Pavilion but the professionals were obliged to come out of a small building at the side, so Patsy came out alone and Percy walked over to him and beckoned him to join the gentlemen, an action much frowned upon by the authorities. On another occasion, when working as an articled clerk I was with a colleague called Gunn. He said, 'Let's go to Lords to see Nottinghamshire play Middlesex' adding that he had a cousin playing for Notts. At lunch he took me to meet all the players and introduced me to Harold Larwood. For a fast bowler he was neither tall nor broad and was a most pleasant man, rather meek and not at all what I imagined. Yet Harold was both famous and feared throughout the world, and much criticised for his body-line bowling in Australia, which caused diplomatic ructions between the two countries. Douglas Jardine, the English captain was equally criticised for ordering the tactic. He wanted to win by whatever means possible, which begs the question; is it better to win or come second with a cheerful smile?

Now football - my life has been dominated by two institutions, about which I am almost obsessed, Arsenal Football Club and Uppingham School. When I was young I did not support any particular team. When Arsenal played Aston Villa in the semi-final of the FA Cup I decided to follow the winner; thus I became an Arsenal fan. Originally they were based south of the river at Woolwich and did not achieve success until 1930 when Herbert Chapman became Manager. He formerly had managed Huddersfield who won the League three times. His impact at Highbury was amazing and under him, and later George Allison, they were League Champions for four years out of five up to 1936, and they won the Cup twice. They were the world's number one team and when England played Italy, one of the few internationals in those days, there were seven Arsenal players in the team. The Scotsman Alex James was their finest player. I considered there would never be a greater manager for Arsenal than Herbert or a player better than Alex. It is only after seventy years and the arrival of Arsene Wegner and Thierry Henry that I have had to revise my views. From boyhood and into my twenties I watched Arsenal on Saturday afternoons as often as I could. I have only ever visited three other grounds. Once to Bury at Gigg Lane, when stationed nearby in the Army, once to Stamford bridge with a Heath Mount friend Barden and also to White hart Lane with Peter Young whose father, Robert I was in partnership with in the fifties. This last time I saw little of the game as I was positioned behind a pillar. This did not concern me as Tottenham were Arsenal's enemies. Gary Porter, a friend of mine in Suffolk, and I visited the Chelsea ground recently and I was amazed to see the luxurious conditions, having only known the crude stands of the Arsenal in the 1930s. I would like to see the new Emirates Stadium, which I have only seen during construction.

I am as keen on Horse Racing, the sport of kings, as on the other three sports. My maternal great-grandfather Graham introduced it to me when I was eleven in 1926 when we went to Sandown Park, the prettiest of all racecourses. I can still remember the rhododendrons. I placed a bet on Southampton, which duly won. Although keen on the sport the only other occasion in the last century I visited a course was to Newmarket in 1937 with Aliki. My great grandfather also used to take David and I for a walk on a Sunday morning and leave us outside the Old Bull and Bush pub. The pub is still there and famous for the song of the last century-Down at the Old Bull and Bush.

This century I have notched up three more meetings; twice to Newmarket with my then neighbour Danny Hatcher and a most memorable visit he arranged to the Derby at Epsom where we were in the Royal Enclosure and I had an excellent view from the Mound of High Chaparral winning. But I got into trouble when, due to the heat, I took my top hat off and an official came and reminded me that in the presence of the Queen this was not allowed. Thank goodness I did not commit the same faux pas at a Royal Garden Party in the seventies, as it was cooler. I was quite a heavy better in the thirties and fifties but only on the big races. My favourite horse on the flat was the King's Sun Chariot a filly who won all her two-year-old races, then the first two classics and finished her career winning the wartime St. Ledger, when she beat the Derby winner, Watling Street by five lengths. Most people would say that the best flat racer of my time was Mill Reef but I would go for Brigadier Gerard, a horse the same age as Mill Reef but one whose distance is a mile, rather than a mile and a half.

I have never been to a National Hunt meeting, which I regret. Arkle is considered the greatest chaser but I would go back to the thirties to Dorothy Paget's Golden Miller. He won four Cheltenham Gold Cups and would have won a fifth but for the weather when it was cancelled. In those days very good horses did not usually run in the Grand National as the fences were too dangerous but Golden Miller, carrying top weight, won in 1934. The next year he was entered again but, having already shown what he could do, sensibly refused at the first fence. My favourite horse of all time is National

Spirit, a God on four legs, who won the Champion Hurdle twice in the fifties. Today, fifty years later, I think of him with affection every February when the National Spirit Hurdle is run at Fontwell. One of my hobbies is to record the ages of the year's racehorses and, at the year-end; I compare my list with that of the Official Handicapper's; my records go back to 1940. Knowledge of sport is most useful in conversation. History is not as useful as one seldom meets people well-versed in the subject. An exception is my good friend Karen Hunt who is a direct descendent of Napoleon's sister.

I do not know at which age the brain is best at retaining facts and I am not talking about reasoning powers but storing knowledge. I know that at the age of eleven information went into my memory box, which I can recall with ease today. In 1926 I knew every football team in the four leagues and the names of their grounds. I also knew the details of the three amateur leagues, Isthmian, Athenian and Spartan. I knew the names of every cricketer in the County teams, including the initials of the gentlemen players. In those days the professionals had just their surnames listed; if two had the same name then the Christian name was printed at the end. Only the amateurs had their initials shown. Such snobbery has long gone. Today if you mention an amateur cricketer to me the initials automatically pop up, H.J. Enthoven, A.P.F. Chapman, R.W.V. Robins, F.R.G. Chalk. When I was twelve my old Headmaster, the Revd 'ARK' Wells drummed history dates into me. Only the other day the Battle of Tenchebrae cropped up and immediately 1106 came to mind. I know little about the battle except its date but it was between Henry I and the French. To divert slightly on this subject may I record a little vignette to show that this subject is not boring. Eleanor of Aquitaine was married to Louis VII, King of France. As she only produced two daughters he divorced her and she then married Henry of Anjou who became Henry II of England, one of our greatest Kings, and she produced four sons and three daughters.

Too many sons as, aided by their mother, the four rebelled against their father and Henry had to lock Eleanor up. If this were fiction people would say it was too farfetched. I would like to look back and take an overview of the great friendships that I have been lucky enough to enjoy in life. Neville Southwell, who died aged 76 in 1992, has been covered in the chapter on Heath Mount. Donald Gourlay and I saw a lot of each other just after prep school and later on he was a great drinking companion. After the war he went to Canada and died tragically young from a mystery infection aged only 36. It is amazing to think that I have outlived him by 57 years and he still remains fresh in my memory, as if it was only yesterday.

Peter Ginsberg and I were brought together over our love of cricket and our friendship continued in the London nightclubs. I last saw Peter in the 1990s when Dorothy and I visited him and his wife at a pub in Sussex. He still liked a drink and he told Dorothy I had changed because I had given up drinking when driving. He died six years later and I still keep in touch with his widow. Although Roy Booth was not a close friend at Heath Mount we did become close friends after I left Uppingham including Heath Mount friends, John Davies and John Sherriff, I kept up with all three for fifty years. Uppingham did not produce so many long lasting friendships, mainly because we were all dispersed by such long distances, but two great friends did emerge, Fred Tordoff and Percy Kennedy. Percy was a good chum at school and we shared a fondness for gambling on the horses and we are still in contact. Fred died in about 2004.

May I finish this chapter with a description of a Treasure Hunt that I and some friends organised in Hampstead? There were twelve teams each with a car and we set about twenty tasks involving finding some information or bringing back some object. I can recall three of the tasks –

- A mischievous one, a phone number was given and the contestants had to phone up and say, 'Are you asleep?' and guess the name of the person answering. Poor Mrs Sleap went ex-directory after this experience.

- The hair of a dog had to be acquired. The contestants were provided with scissors and had to snip at some poor hapless hound being taken for a walk.

- This one was my idea – the contestants had to persuade a blonde, who was unknown to them to get in their car and join them at the finishing post. We had a good collection of blondes at the end.

Grandparents & Father
Germany, 1906

Nurse Robinson (Birds & Bees)

Grandmother & Alaric

Alaric

Avening House 1917, outside greenhouse. Back Row: Margaret,
Hilda, Winifred, Father. Front Row: Grandfather, Alaric, Mother,
Grandmother and a reluctant Douglas.

Father

Avening House. Hampstead

NEW WAREHOUSES AND OFFICES, ST. JOHN STREET, WEST SMITHFIELD.—Mr. Lewis H. Isaacs, A. R. I. B. A.

Farmiloe's business, St Jhons Street, West Smithfield

Douglas, Brussels C. 1921, aged 6yrs

Margaret & Winifred
Skiing

Ceremony of Grandfather given Freedom of Southwold, May 1920. Grandfather not present but Howard in background.

Garden at Avening House

Sothwold Railway. closed C. 1929

Grandfather & Douglas setting off for a bathe in Southwold with an alternative
use of bathing huts with Mr Smith and Tom Palmer

Mr Smith, standing by his Southwold Beach Hut

Tom Palmer outside his hut in Southwold

Chambers next to 'Lancia'

Alaric taking Hilda for a ride

Henstead Hall 1960 when we moved in.
Notice no driveway at the time

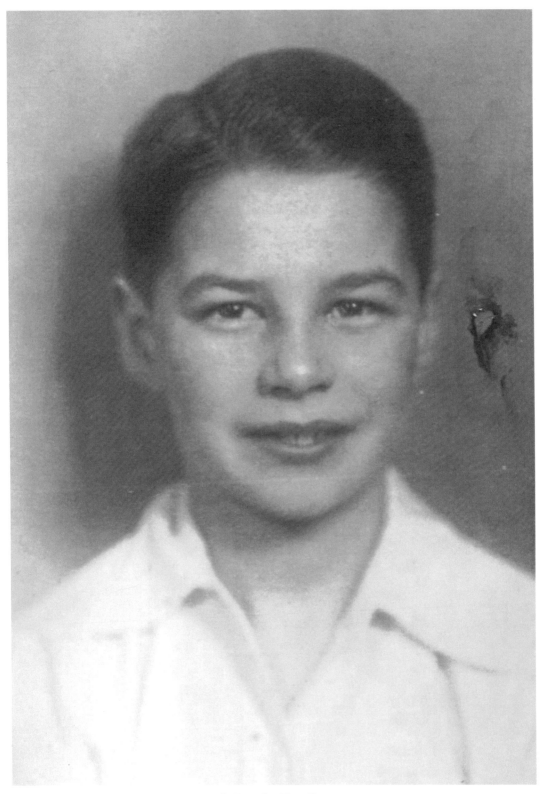

G. Douglas Farmiloe
Feb. 1928

Portrait of R. H. Owen
painted by Howard Speed

Uppingham Memorial Hall and Classrooms

Aliki
kindly sent by her family

Aliki, taken in a village in France on
the way Juan Les Pins. 1937

The only picture I have of my 1936 'SS1 Jaguar' taken outside 16 Orchardleigh Shanklin. (Auntie's House)

Douglas beside
Fathers grave in
Moray Cemetery

Douglas with son Michael and
daughter Susan C. 2000

Douglas & Dorothy
Orient Express 1991

LasVegas 2004

Douglas in Las Vegas on his 95th birthday, in favourite bar (Napoleon's Champagne Bar, Paris, Vegas) with Grandson Lewis & Sheba.

March 2010 with my Great
Grandaughter Susan

July 2010 standing by Rolls Royce with Helen & Sheba

CHAPTER SIX

A Mayfair Playboy

(And the Love of my Life)

It was one summer's day in 1932 that I first met Aliki Psychopoulos, a girl who was to play such a large part in my life, and to this day still is in my thoughts. The big house, Oakley Court, an imposing mansion in well-maintained grounds was occupied by Mr Olivier, an Armenian millionaire and his family. He sent a note down to Shirley inviting his son and nephew to come up and play tennis with his daughter and a school friend. David and I put on our white flannels; in those days people did not yet wear shorts, and with our racquets under our arms strolled along the towpath to the Court. We were slightly nervous, as we had never met the young ladies who were at a finishing school in Switzerland. On arrival we introduced ourselves. The parents were away but there were plenty of maids supplying drinks and later, tea. I was seventeen and the girls a few months younger. Mireille Olivier had a pale olive skin, pretty, round face and was rather on the plump side. I have always liked skinny girls, unlike the Middle Eastern taste, which is for a more voluptuous girl, and it was her friend Aliki that bowled me over; Aliki was quite natural and at once put David and I at our ease. The reader must remember that I was very young and, up until now, had had little contact with girls. The sisters of prep school friends had been ignored, as boys then did not play with girls. Uppingham was so male-dominated that it could have been a monastery. Fred Tordoff had an older sister but in fact much too older to be of use. Girlfriends were seldom discussed by Uppingham boys, although John McIver, who was a few years older than I claimed he had a fiancé. Film Stars were the exception to this rule. Actresses mesmerised us. My favourites were Laura La Plante and the 'It' girl, Clara Bow and then to top them all, Janet Gaynor. I still have her signed photograph on the cabinet in my front room and am looking at it now. Janet took over from Mary Pickford as the world's sweetheart. In 1928 she was the first actress to win an Oscar in those days the award was given for films produced during that year and not as the case today of one individual film. Janet made three films during that year of which the best known Is Seventh Heaven. In 1937 she starred in the first version of 'A Star Is Born' and was nominated for best actress. Many years later I saw her on television but the years had made their mark and she had grown tubby. Her ending was sad; she and Mary Martin were in a taxi when it crashed. Mary was injured but Janet suffered worse and was to die two years later in 1984 caused by the accident. But we must return to that tennis court by the side of the Thames. David was not a strong player, nor Mireille, I was quite good and Aliki excellent. I cannot remember the pairings but the afternoon was a success. I was smitten and had high hopes for another meeting but this was not to be until three years later, and other heartthrobs had passed my way.

I was living in a flat in Belsize Park when there was a telephone call. It was Aliki. Her father ran an import/export business and the family were well off. Her life in England was confined to the small UK-Greek community and then she spent time abroad at school or in Greece. She had little contact with the world outside these confines. Then one day she met Primrose Dain, perhaps at a local tennis club, and they became close friends, shopping together and meeting up at each other's houses. Primrose was upper middle-class, she was the youngest of three sisters, all of whom had been debutantes and presented at Court. Though not necessarily attractive, and with an aquiline nose, Primrose was witty and had boundless enjoyment of life. I can remember some of her phrases, a visit to the dentist's involved, 'pulling tuskies,' and when the evening was getting on and some people wanted to go home, she would entice them to stay, saying, 'The night is still a pup'. Primrose and I got on excellently. The last time I saw her was just after the war at Golders Green station. I had my bowler and rolled umbrella heading for my office and she was primly dressed going to hers. She was still unmarried and the effervescence had gone. I understood the war had been a sobering influence on her. Primrose would invite Aliki to cocktail and other parties but she had no escort. Then, remembering the tennis game of three years earlier, I came to mind. She tracked me down via the Olivier's, Uncle Shirley and Dodie, but at first I was hesitant, not being keen on parties where I would know hardly anyone. But I went along and after a few happenings I got to know the people and Aliki even better. By the time my twenty first birthday party came along we were good friends but no more than that.

At this time I was hard up. I could not afford to run a car and my only income was an allowance from Budgie and the odd tenner at Christmas from Jocelyn, Miles and Page. I worked, but for no pay. So Aliki and I had to go by foot to parties but on the way back, if we did not get a lift, we took a taxi. On other occasions we would, slightly tipsy, negotiate the Central and Piccadilly Lines back to Notting Hill Gate. We were both shy and unless I knew many people at a gathering I was ill at ease but we soon found our feet and would be at home at the smartest establishments. Aliki had the looks and poise to pass anywhere and, unless you actually knew she was Greek, you would consider her English. Her mastery of our language was amazing and only occasionally would she ask me what a word meant, but, living in the world she did, she could be snobbish; She could recognise one's accent as to whether they went to Public School and if they did not he was not a gentleman. During these two following years we gave each other terrific mutual support; never in my whole life have I achieved such a rapport with anyone, something I will never forget. I can recall no argument; we always were honest with each other; for instance she said she would never be able to marry me. My only regret is that I have never found anyone else in life that was so close.

It was sometime after my twenty first birthday, about May 1936, that Aliki and I began to see a lot of each other. Firstly I had to buy a car and also, which took a little time, to lay my hands on my inheritance. Then we saw each other every day until my return from our trip to the French Riviera, when she stayed on. When Aliki did get back to town we picked up as before, seeing each other every day. We were still going strong at the end of 1937, the climax of which was the Chelsea Arts Ball on New Year's Eve. The fight with Neville Southwell over her would have taken place early in 1938 and also later Rene Thompson appeared on the scene. I never lost touch with her until 1963, we never had a quarrel, and after the first great passions had died down a strong bond remained.

Once at the height of the affair she phoned my mother asking to go and see her while I was at work. She told her she was concerned lest I was falling in love, adding she could never marry me, and asking mother not to tell me about the visit. Dodie kept quiet but of course Aliki could not and she told me all that evening. The problem was that being Greek she was expected to marry another Greek. There was an older cousin, Costa, who she had met in Greece when at an impressionable age and she had fallen head over heels in love with him – he must have appeared like a Greek God to her. Although she never saw him during our time his presence was keenly felt and I was very much an 'also ran'. My position could be likened to the subject of the Al Bowly song, which he sang with Ray Noble's Orchestra,

You may not be an angel

Because angels are so few

But until one comes along

I'll string along with you.

On one occasion her uncle came over from Greece. He was staying at the Mount Royal Hotel in Marble Arch and asked his beautiful niece out to dinner and later drinks in his room. Then he tried to ravage her and she had to make a hasty exit. The following evening she confided this all to me; another example of how close we were and how we had no secrets from each other.

Where were the haunts of the jeunesse of the 1930s? Most of them I visited with Aliki, the more seedy ones without her. Sometimes we went to The Nest in Kingley Street, on occasions I would go there at 4 am, having dropped her home. Then there was The Nineteenth in Cork Street, a day club and quite respectable. It was here that the notorious gang of Public School jewel thief's met after their robbery. This event took place in 1937 and which shook the whole country. Four young 'Men about Town' who found themselves short of money hatched a ridiculous plot to carry out a jewel robbery. They were Robert Harley, David Wilmer, John Lonsdale, a Canadian and Peter Jenkins, an Old Harrovian. Jenkins who booked a suite of rooms in the Hyde Park Hotel and then telephoned Cartier's asking them to send up a selection of rings on approval. Mr Etienne Bellinger, their Manager duly arrived with £16,000 worth of rings. The robbers did not intend to use force but things got out of hand. All four were tanked up with alcohol and just as Mr Bellinger came into the room Robert Harley, wearing a mask, rushed in and coshed him and he fell seriously wounded. The four grabbed the rings and fled to a nearby flat. Later that evening they assembled in The Nineteenth Club to distribute the spoils. I was not in The Nineteenth that evening but I knew Harley and Wilmer well and the robbery was the talk of the town and I soon heard all about it. The Press had a field day and the four criminals were soon caught and sentenced at the Old Bailey, Harley got seven years and the cat of nine tails, Wilmer five years and the cat, Jenkins three years and Lonsdale eighteen months with hard labour.

When I first took Aliki out she had just one evening dress and the colour was blue, and she looked very pretty in it. She could not wear it every night and she persuaded her father to buy her a white one. In the end there was quite a collection; she must have proved an expensive daughter. My outfits were expensive as well. I had three dress suits, single-breasted, double-breasted and tails. I had a good camel hair coat and a pair of musquash gloves for driving, costing three guineas, £150 in today's money, and one of them got lost. For accessories I would raid the stock of my men's outfitter's shop and so I had silk shirts, ties from Scheperelli etc. It was bad form to have ones bow tie ready- made and I was inept at tying mine, but my shop was just across the road from my flat, and my manager, Johnson conveniently did it for me. Aliki and I did not spend all our time in nightclubs; we played a lot of tennis at her club. The man, all things being equal, should beat the girl, but I had to struggle to win the sets, the score invariably being 6-4, or 7-5. Once I had been accepted by her parents as part of the scenery we played contract bridge at their house, 7 Dawson Place, Bayswater. With my head for figures I was a fair player and her parents who played most evenings were exceedingly good; Aliki, who was brought up with the game was good as well, so I was the weak link in the four, but if I made a mistake this never led to arguments.

I passed my driving test in 1936. The system was in its infancy and I recall my instructor telling me to memorise the number plates of the cars standing in the centre car park. The examiner took me to the balcony and asked me to read the numbers out. As it was I could read them but a short-sighted driver with a good memory could have passed this hurdle as well. My driving school had four instructors, there was no rush to teach me, but all four were anxious to teach Aliki when I paid for her to take lessons. Dodie knew Aliki well and I took her down to Henstead Hall to meet Budgie. Also I recall inviting my old music master, R.G.Oakley, the one I used to play up at Uppingham, and who was now head of music at Bishops Stortford College, to make up a four at bridge with my mother. My motives were to show off Aliki, whenever she was there my ego was boosted; she was the centre of my life.

I would like to sketch some of our favourite venues and highlight the incidents that occurred there. Quaglino's was a favourite of ours and is still going strong today. I was there once with Aliki and the band was playing 'Cheek to Cheek', one of my favourites; I always liked dancing cheek to cheek with her. Then, just as we were leaving the dance floor I spied Uncle Shirley with one of his lady friends. We had a chat and I was delighted to show Aliki off and he was somewhat surprised to see his young nephew as a man about town. The Cafe de Paris was another favourite and I remember it well. You walked down a flight of stairs to a small dance floor and the band was on a platform on the left hand side. We would often dine in hotels. There were the Cafe Royal and The Trocadero off Piccadilly, and The Mayfair and The Berkeley, where The Berkeley Buttery was good for a cheerful meal. But our favourites were in Park Lane, The Dorchester and The Grosvenor House. The Dorchester was our local and I recall Aliki saying one evening, 'You know Douglas, we are always the youngest people here'. I suppose most of our friends found The Dorchester rather expensive. Another evening there was a raffle and I won the prize, a large photo of Aliki by a society photographer. My first wife set fire to it. Should I go back to The Dorchester one day or will I be disturbed there by the ghosts of the past? The price of a set dinner was 21/-, so with drinks, cocktails and tips your bill would be some 70/- for the evening, £170 in today's money. If you wanted to save money there was The Mayfair at 17/6 a head.

Among the restaurants we used to visit was The Lansdown House, which is still in existence. The Cafe de Paris was a favourite place for dinner and dance. The bandleader there was Snake Hips Johnson, a sleek, good looking West Indian with a charming smile and all the ladies fell for him. I got to know him well and sometimes gave him a bottle of wine, but even without this inducement he would play our favourite Fred Astaire and Ginger Rogers tunes. It was advertised as the safest place in the West End, but this did not prevent a bomb falling right through the entrance killing thirty people. Al Bowly had a lucky escape, being out of town that night. Snake Hips Johnson was also killed by the bomb on that night, Al Bowly was killed by a bomb outside his flat in Jermyn Street. There were many famous advertised dance bands in the thirties, Harry Roy, Roy Fox, Bert Ambrose, Ray Noble, Carol Gibbons, Joe Loss, Jack Payne and Jack Hilton. An excellent, cosy and select eating place was The Coq D'Or in Jermyn Street, which is still going today and there was a good place opposite; was it The Kit Kat Club? I would occasionally visit The Hungaria in Lower Regent Street, but in those days there were far fewer Continental and Asian restaurants; there were some in Soho and there was a smart Indian one, Veeraswamy's, just off Regent Street which is still there. The Lyons' Group had a chain of restaurants called Corner Houses and the waitresses, who wore smart outfits, were called 'Nippies'. Their flagship was The Cumberland in Marble Arch. The Corner Houses were the up and coming places for the masses, not for us, although I did meet my second wife in a Corner House and once I ventured into one with Aliki and some of her girlfriends; we were so noisy that we were thrown out.

Occasionally Aliki and I decided we wanted to get away from it all so we drove out of town to a roadside pub. The Spiders Web, outside Watford, was one of our favourites; another was The Berkeley Arms at Heathrow, which in fact was a hotel with turrets. Many years later, on the way to the States with Dorothy my wife, we decided to stay the night there. The taxi driver could not find it and just drove around in circles. Then I spotted the turrets. The building was there with a new name.

There was an extra advantage of these country visits; our good night kiss, which could last half an hour and took place in a country lane. When we were in town I would park in a side road just off Dawson Place where she lived but of course the country was far more romantic.

The modern party-goer will be surprised to know that in the thirties there were night clubs that operated in the day. I suppose there were more 'idle rich' then. The doors would open at 11am and close at midnight, when habitués could move onto the real nightclubs. A favourite one of our circle was in Knightsbridge. Sadly I cannot remember its name; the decor was nothing special but the place had just the right atmosphere. The proprietress decided to capitalise on her success and moved to a smarter premises nearby, but the atmosphere had gone and we all stayed away. It was at this establishment that I had my celebrated fight with Neville Southwell over Aliki. As I have already mentioned this never interfered with our lifelong friendship.

There was a club in Cork Street called The Nineteenth to which Donald Gourlay introduced me. I recall one of my drinking friends there was Simon Bonham-Carter, a scion of the well-known family, and relative of the actress Helena. He was a little bit older than me and had receding hair. Donald was one of my more raffish friends and he involved me in a curious incident. There was a Hollywood film star staying in London and, not thinking much of English girls, he sent for his girlfriend from the States. Donald had offered to collect her from the airport, but his Bentley was in for repairs, so I was asked to do the run and I was warned to be on good behaviour and not make a pass. In fact I was never tempted as she turned out to be a big, busty, buxom, platinum blond who kept calling me 'Honey'. I was more than relieved when I had discharged my duty.

There was a ritual with nightclubs, which had to be followed so as to comply with the licensing laws. The pretence was that a bottle party was going on and then you had to sign a chit to say you were a member and had ordered a bottle of spirits the day before. Mrs Meyrick was the nightclub queen in the decade before mine and it was her cavalier attitude to these rules that was forever landing her in jail; this did not stop her three daughters all marrying peers.

There were four main nightclubs at the top of Aliki's and my list. The first two were the The Paradise and The Coconut Grove both in Regent Street. Most of the hostesses, which crop up in my story were to be found here. If you strolled down Regent Street during the day they were so inconspicuous that you would not know they were there. At night they came to life. Also there were so few cars around that you could park down the centre of Regent Street without trouble, only once was mine ever towed away. Once inside one found dim lights, plush furnishings and comfy sofas. Sandwiches were available and in the early hours, eggs and bacon. The hostesses were paid a commission on what you spent but if you were in a mixed party they were not involved. A band provided the music and there was also Cabaret; in this informal atmosphere you could chat with the stars. Their fame has faded but they were a great draw for the clientele. I recall the names of Edward Arnold and Norman Long. Norman had a song, My Little Austin Seven, the gist of which was that the Austin Seven was so small that you could park it under the stairs. Another star was Douglas Byng, a female impersonator and comedian who had an international reputation. I recall chatting to an American, Harry Richmond, whose most famous song which is still sung today, was Putting on the Ritz. King Farook was often a guest, then a slim lad of eighteen, later he became extremely fat. Aliki and I would go to a club about three times a week.

The other two of our favourites were the particularly select Florida and the most exclusive of all, The 400 Club. When Mark Birley founded Annabel's in the sixties, it was on the site of The 400 Club. One other club that should not be forgotten was The White Monkey but this was not a nightclub.

The Nest in Kingley Street was very popular. Aliki and I did occasionally go there together but usually I would call in at 4am after dropping her home. All the management and staff were black and the top black artists came over from the States. There was a waiter called Sam who always went out of his way to find me a good table; he was so helpful but then I was a good tipper. I recall going to a nightclub where Nat Gonella was playing. His singer Moya Stella insisted on dancing with me and there was some hanky panky. Nat was furious and became aggressive, not surprisingly – she was his girl. They later married but I note they were divorced in 1942.

It was not only in the evening I was with Aliki; we would have tea at Fortnum and Mason's. I took her to Henley to see my great aunt Popsy, of whom I was very fond. She was then in her late seventies and lived into her nineties, putting her longevity down to a few cigarettes and some whisky each day. We were at the 1936 Wimbledon Final when Budge beat the German, Von Cram. At Newmarket we ran into Len Osgerby, the fine Old Uppinghamian Rugby player. He was very good looking and Aliki asked where I had been hiding him. He sadly died of wounds in 1940, only 23 years old. My recollections of the day were clear; the two-year old races were won by Midday Sun and Exhibitionist. The next year they won the Derby and The Oakes respectively.

I remember well Aliki's twenty first Birthday Party at her parent's house in Dawson Place. You went down steps from the front door to the ground floor where there was a large room leading into the garden. Most of the guests were Greeks whom I did not know. She poured the drinks out while I handed them around and I had time to steal a few kisses by the shrubbery while I did so. I was relieved when I could escape and go to a Night Club.

Each of Aliki's girlfriends came from a different country. We have met Mireille, who was Armenian and Primrose who was English. Dodd was Australian, about six feet tall, with a brother at Oxford, the only time I ever went there was to visit him. Franca Torricelli was Italian, eighteen and very attractive. Once I gave her a lift back to her flat and we could not resist a kiss. She told Aliki and I was in deep trouble. Hers was one of the leading families of Milan. Primrose lived around the corner from Aliki and I often went around there in the daytime, when I met her mother. Once I met Pat, her elder sister, who was about twenty six. She was more mature than us and I have never met such an elegant and beautiful woman. When introduced I was mesmerized and then she teased me about this in the nicest way.

The Cambridge May Balls for Undergraduates and their friends were great fun. The first one I went to was in 1936 when I was twenty one at the invitation of Neville Southwell who was at Christ Church. I booked into The University Arms, the best hotel in Cambridge for two nights, but in fact only spent one there. I danced the evening away with a charming girl who said she wanted to see me again. So that I would not forget her name she wrote it in ink on the cuff of my dress shirt. She had written Lady Margaret Hall. This must have been the name of her college. Everyone was very drunk yet Neville and his friends gathered on the College lawns for more. I recall one hearty called Symes-Thompson who was taking the Mickey out of me. I chatted back and for some reason he thought my repartee quite funny and sophisticated and he told Neville what a great chap I was. This could not have been the case at the time as I lacked confidence and was quite green behind the ears. It just shows how the prism of alcohol can affect judgements. That night I slept on the college floor; we were all too drunk to go anywhere else. Neville invited me again with a telegram the next year, saying, 'Short of girls for the Ball, bring as many as you can'. As well as Aliki I must have taken her friends, Primrose and Mireille, Franca would have been in Italy at the time. On the way back at 4 am the Jag broke down just by a lorry driver's all-night cafe. There were terrific catcalls when three young ladies and myself in evening dresses walked in. My charges were most embarrassed and Mireille was particularly worried about what her parents would think, but no doubt when they look back they saw the funny side.

I must say a few words about Janette. She was a brunette and very petite; always dressed to perfection, without a hair out of place. She was a good friend of mine and Aliki's and always had two men to accompany her. She was like a piece of china, so delicate that if you touched her she would break. She always fitted in and was most pleasant. One day none of her men friends were around to take her home so I offered and she asked me in for coffee. Once inside she transformed into something very passionate; I was astounded by the transformation but I resisted an entanglement, as Aliki was so important.

Primrose's boyfriend was a captain in the tank corps and she was staying nearby his base with relatives in Folkestone. She invited Aliki and I for the weekend and we stayed at The Grand Hotel. On the Saturday evening we met in the hotel bar and each of us consumed six white ladies, a popular cocktail of the day consisting of gin, cointreau and lemon juice. It is not widely available today but it is well worth trying, but I would not advise six of them. When the Captain arrived we were plastered and he asked if we had ever driven in a tank. We had not so he drove us to his camp in Lydd at one in the morning, we got in and off we went. In fact we were very hungry as we had had no dinner and on the way back to Folkestone we stopped at an all night cafe and enjoyed one of the best bacon and eggs I have ever tasted. Many years later my wife Dorothy and I decided to go to Paris by hovercraft so I left my Rolls in The Grand's car park where we stayed the night. The car was quite safe, protected by the car parks high netting but I had not accounted for the red dust that can be drummed up on the South Coast. So much had fallen on the car it was a different colour.

Aliki's parents had friends in Chamonix in the French Alps but as they did not have a car I offered to drive them there and the plan was to go to the Riviera first. Off we set in the Jag, the first stop Paris. It was the only time I have driven in Paris itself and in 1937 there were fewer cars about. The parents were very easy going on the trip; her father spoke some English and they found the back seat of the Jag comfortable. In Paris Aliki and I visited a smart Russian nightclub, The Casanova, and drank out of golden goblets. The drive down to the South was leisurely and before long we were in Juan Les Pins. We visited Cannes and Nice, and Monte Carlo for some gaming, and also Antibes, the favourite of London society. It was like home from home and we made for the exclusive Eden Roc club, built on a promontory. Aliki was a good swimmer and I was not. The reader will remember that I had to struggle to pass the test at Uppingham. We swam out to the rock and then rested. I dreaded the return swim, but with her help I made it, but did not recover my composure until after a few cocktails.

After a few days we drove to Chamonix and stayed in a hotel before I had to return to England. My heart was heavy, as I had to leave Aliki behind. Just before the holiday I met a girl at a party, her name has been lost in the mists of time, but after a few drinks we got on well. She said she was going to Baden Baden with her parents and I said I would call in if I was passing. My knowledge of European geography was hazy and I had not realised it was so far but the trip was interesting; I drove the whole length of Switzerland and into the Black Forest. I recall stopping for a meal in Geneva and thinking it was the cleanest city I had ever seen. Aliki told me I was stupid to call on a girl I hardly knew and she was right; it turned out that without the alcohol she had no fascination, but her parents were very kind, glad to have some company for their daughter, and we all dined together. The Hotel Stephanie in Baden Baden was a splendid building but I noticed we only had a tiny portion of butter. Hitler had decreed that guns came before butter. It should have been clear to all that with his rearmament campaign he had no intention of peace. I could not see how Chamberlain could have been so naive to be hoodwinked by Hitler. Firm early action could have prevented the carnage that followed, but I am criticising with hindsight. Pitt the Younger, perhaps our greatest Prime Minister, appeased the French after their Revolution and so did not prevent the Anglo-French wars of 1793-1815. What if Pitt had taken firm action from the start, the Revolution could have been nipped in the bud, the Monarch restored and Napoleon's career never got off the ground. But I must return from this sojourn into European history to pre-war France. On the way back I went down a one-way street the wrong way in Strasburg and was stopped by a Policeman. We had no common language and when he worked out I was English, knowing we were all mad, let me go.

Back to life in England, I booked two tickets for the Chelsea Arts Ball, which was to be held on New Year's Eve, 1936. It was a most fashionable event. I had always enjoyed good health, only a bout of Rheumatic Fever held me up when I was young. But on December 30th I was down with 'flu and on the 31ˢᵗ I was unable to leave my bed. What a tragedy! I telephoned Aliki asking her to collect the tickets as they were expensive and should not be wasted, and the good news is that she found an escort. It wasn't Neville; perhaps it was John Dickson, another Old Uppinghamian who was a close friend of ours. I did not know him at all at school as he was four terms ahead, but now we were often at the same parties. At that time he had no idea of what he wanted to do. As it was he joined the Artist Rifles, a select Public School Territorial Unit. I joined as well but I did not stay as it took up too much time, but John had found his vocation, served as a Commando in the War in Burma and Madagascar, winning the DSO and bar and retiring as a Lieutenant Colonel. I was not worried that she would be led astray by her escort as at that time we could not have been closer, but the whole saga did not improve my condition.

At the next years Chelsea Arts Ball there were no hiccups. It was a very grand affair and we came across a lot of my Farmiloe cousins who had a box. Princess Marina, who was Greek, was there, which thrilled Aliki. She was most elegant, royal, but did not appear to be enjoying herself. Her playboy husband, the Duke of Kent, was; but the star of the evening was Merle Oberon, who stood out above all others.

Were the girls of the thirties any different to those of today? I think the ones I knew had as much freedom, independence, ability to drink and have a good time as any today. The First World War was the great watershed, leading to the Charleston, the Black Bottom, and the Eton Crop of the flappers. All this went on against the background of the poverty of the masses, highlighted by the Jarrow March. The big difference between the girls of the thirties and those of today is that they drew the line at 'going all the way'. Indeed Aliki was no exception and being continental she was stricter. We trusted each other, knew the boundaries and kept to them. Our goodnight embraces might take half an hour. I would park my car around the corner from Dawson Place; the gear stick was an encumbrance so we moved to the back seat. I used to take Aliki home before midnight and waited round the corner, her parents by then were asleep and she crept out of the house. I returned her about 3.00-4.00am most nights. This went on for a year until one day her father was not feeling very well, the tablets he required were in Aliki's room, but of course, she wasn't there. Next morning a frantic call from Aliki asking me to go round. It wasn't as bad as I expected as neither parents spoke too much English (the mother less). I think that her father would have accepted me as a son-in-law but definitely not her mother. The outcome was that we didn't have to pretend any more and we came back later. We still had our half hour cuddle on the side road.

Once a Policeman knocked on the window and asked if we were alright, 'Yes, Officer', I replied. He said he was sorry to disturb us and said goodnight. Had we in fact gone 'all the way' it would have been her duty to marry me. We were on that threshold twice. There was an evening in a county lane near The Spiders Web, the next day she said, 'I wanted you to go all the way last night'. The other time was in the Paris Hotel on the way to the South of France. She knocked on my door in the middle of the night asking to come in. My habit was to lock the door and after the drinks at The Casanova I was sleeping soundly, and slept on. Had the dice rolled differently on these two occasions the course of my life would have been different. After Neville came on the scene with Aliki our paths still crossed as we went in the same circle. Our friendship had become platonic, I had moved on with other girls. Neville and Aliki were tense for a time but he never had any more chance than I did with Aliki's fascination for Costa.

I was married in October 1938 and I wanted to see what Aliki thought of my new wife, Pat. The new bride created no difficulties and they had tea at Fortnum's. I phoned Aliki afterwards for her verdict, 'quite a nice girl, pretty, but you have married out of your class.' I knew she would say this. Pat would create more than just difficulties later when in a fit of spirited jealousy she tore up the expensive Dorchester picture. She also destroyed an equally expensive one of Rene, whom you will meet later. When war broke out Aliki and her family moved to Alton in Hampshire. In June 1942 she married another Greek, one with an unpronounceable name, John Karaiossifoglou of the Royal Hellenic Navy. A daughter was born the following July, Lelia, who announced her engagement in The Times in 1964 to Rouilly Vaganas of Athens. John had then died and Aliki had remarried and was Mrs Nigel Turner of Princes Gate Court, Kensington. Eleven years later, in 1975, Lelia's brother also named John announced his engagement.

Aliki must then have died as the notice said 'the late Mrs A Turner'. I last saw her in 1963 and we had a long chat about old times. She asked if I liked the new dances like the Cha Cha, I replied saying no, not ever having been a great dancer and only just managing the Fox Trot or a poor Waltz. She asked if I still had the picture of her on the Jag. I did then, kept with her last letter of the mid 60's, but I have now lost it. I used to hide such things in client's old accountancy files and when we moved offices a lot of them were burnt. Luckily I still have a picture of her taken in France, which I have enlarged. The last letter said she was leaving London for Athens and invited Dorothy and I to stay there. Dorothy and I did in fact go to Athens twice but never called; just as well as there could have been a row. I had an address and phone number; she asked me to keep an eye on her son who had just taken up articles with the Chartered Accountants, Price Waterhouse. I did not in fact follow things up as we were living in the country and Dorothy may have been jealous. I have since then, with no luck, tried to pick up the trail. There were a few Turners at Price Waterhouse but such a search is a hopeless task with no Christian name. The Greek Embassy could not help, nor a Turner living in Athens. I last saw Neville in 1989. We called in at his house in Turners Hill, Crawley. Neville was enjoying his drinks and also kept filling up Dorothy with gin, much of which she sensibly decanted into a pot plant; there was also a retired headmaster there, a bit tipsy, who took a shine to her.

JOHN & LELIA

It was only at the beginning of February 2010 that I eventually located Aliki's two children. I know now for certain that Aliki had died in 1976 (thirty four years previously). It was masterly detective work that Jacqui was able to find her son on Flickr, in Greece with his wife Ruth supervising the building of their new home in Peloponnese, where they have retired to.

My earlier effects twenty odd years ago hampered by the fact that I did not have access to the Internet and was under the impression that Aliki's Cousin whom she married had the Christian name Karais, which was in effect his Surname. Also Nigel Turner was her Second Husband and I assumed the two children were his. In fact when I first made enquiries Aliki's Son, John was actually living in Suffolk less than ten miles away.

Aliki divorced her Second Husband about 1963 and moved to Greece in 1966. She had two children, Lelia born 1943 and John born five years later. Both were educated in England and John went to a leading public school, Charterhouse.

Neither John or Lelia had ever heard of me but the reception I have received from both, John and Lelia, letters, emails and telephone conversations has been truly marvellous. They have become very good friends whom I hope to meet in the future. Both were interested to know facts about their mother who had died so many years ago. I also learnt many things about Aliki, which I did not know but I have decided not to alter in any way what I have previously written about.

Of course I was able to give information about their grandparents and what was interesting was they both knew Mirielle and Franca who feature in my memoirs.

One fact however I will mention as I had pointed out that Aliki was a good bridge player in fact she was excellent as she won the Greek Ladies Championships three times.

One pleasing postscript to all this. Readers will recall when Aliki, Primrose and I had six 'white ladies' in Folkestone. Lelia and John were in Athens recently and ordered 'white ladies' and drank a toast to Aliki and Douglas. However I gather those 'White Ladies' were not up to the English standard we experienced.

CHAPTER SEVEN
Rene Thompson

I have had five serious relationships in my life and this one without doubt is the most intriguing.

It has puzzled me why I fell in love with Rene, a nightclub hostess, when at the time I was a Mayfair Playboy with many notches on my standard, but, anyhow I did. She was the only hostess whose surname I knew and whenever I hear the song, 'Thanks for the Memory' I think of her with a little sadness. She was a part-time model and added to her income hostessing in The Florida and she had a nice flat in Mapleton House, Leicester Square. I went to The Florida one evening without Aliki and sat with a girl with red hair.

So on that particular night I arrived at the Florida with a party and we sat down at a table waiting for our drinks, which of course had to be a bottle ordered the day before to make it legal. Of course one only ordered it on entry but the order was dated the day before. The marvellous eggs and bacon the club provided at 4am you did not have to order the day before.

After a time I went to the toilet (of course then and now the correct word in Upper Society is lavatory). On the way back there was a hostess on a table waiting to be booked when I spotted Rene. I left the group and booked this glamorous girl and we had a table to ourselves. By that time I had had my fair share of drinks i.e cocktails, wine and the whiskey. I had to order a bottle. I didn't want spirits and I don't think wine was ever served at bottle parties. It had to be champagne. That would have lasted the evening for us. Hostesses received a commission from the club when their client ordered a drink and champagne paid the largest commission. On top of that the customer was expected to pay the hostess for sitting with her till the early hours of the morning. She would have reaped more if she took him home to her flat.

On that first night I was well inebriated. I told her I was in love with her and she was the most adorable girl in the World and was able to get a few kisses in. I wasn't asked back to her flat and in any case probably wouldn't have been any use. I promised to see her the next evening and told her not to take any bookings.

The next morning in the cold light of being sober I was horrified by my action. My darling Aliki was due back very shortly and I felt I had let her down badly. I also let Rene down, as I didn't turn up the next evening. That was the end of the matter with Rene at least for the time being. Months passed and 1938 had arrived and Neville and Aliki had become an item.

I met Rene a second time in 1938, some few months had elapsed since the previous 1937 meeting and I was no longer an item with Aliki. I don't recall if I happened to be with a party at the Florida or else I had decided to see her again. Anyway I joined her at the table and considering she must have sat with umpteen men during the last eight months or so was flattered that she remembered me very well but also she remembered I had let her down. I had to do some apologising but there were no hard feelings. In fact we got on extremely well and I was certainly less inebriated this time round. This time I said I would definitely see her the next evening. I don't know whether she thought I would turn up or not. I do know however that she didn't ask me back to her flat that night.

It is certain that I went to the Florida for the next few nights to sit with her and the chemistry would have worked between us. Just like in the case of Pat my memory is completely blank for the first month of our acquaintance so I can only speculate what happened and it is complete guesswork.

We would have drunk champagne and I would have paid her for sitting with me. In this period we would have found we had a lot in common, we would have danced close together and I would have kissed her on the sofa where we sat. I did not go home with her, as I did not know her well enough so it avoided the question of paying for sex. However after a week she had a few days holiday and as by that time we were close I would see her during the daytime and evening. It was during that time that she first asked me to her bed – a pleasure that was to continue for another five to six months.

She did go back to work for about a week after then and I didn't go to the Florida every night. I would see her during the day and perhaps wait for her in her flat until she returned from work.

After that she decided to give up work entirely. She had a comfortable balance in the Bank, as like the majority of hostesses she would have entertained guests from the club, which provided a nest egg. Financially she wouldn't be so well off but she continued with part time modelling and I did help her sometimes with her rent. The flat, Mapleton House is situated near Leicester Square and would have been very expensive. Incidentally the flats are still there as I especially looked for the block as recent as 2007. Apart from these two meetings and my final meeting I can only remember one specific day during that time. I can recall the flat in detail and what happened there, but what, where and when we went, that awful blankness of mind eludes me.

I need to cover six months. I do not remember whom of my circle of friends we met but obviously we did. I have two clues and they go to show we were indeed a couple. Firstly my conversation with my mother, which has given me a lot of information and secondly a letter from Neville Southwell written about six years later when he refers to her, which shows she wasn't just a hostess I picked up for one day.

Before expanding on the flat, I will go through the specific day, which show we were close. Apart from the two nights when I first met Rene and our final meeting I only have a vivid recollection.

One afternoon in 1938 I had a telephone call at the shop. Rene was being harassed by a man and she asked me to go along and say I was her fiancé. Two points here are that I would never have given my business telephone number to anyone unless she was my girlfriend and secondly Rene was in trouble so the one she thought of was myself to rescue her.

When I received the message my first thought was only of her. I think I thought she was my intended I had to rescue her and set out as her knight in shining armour with sword drawn riding a charger to rescue a damsel in distress. On arrival the damsel would swoon in my arms. I was always a romantic but it didn't work out that way at all. instead I drove the Jag to Leicester Square and the journey and parking the car would have taken a full thirty minutes.

I rushed up the stairs at Mapleton House to her flat. I must have had a key to her flat because Rene didn't open the door, she was standing in the middle of the flat a bit dazed. I recall I didn't go straight up to her but walked towards the window, which was opposite her front door. On my right was a fireplace with ornaments (no fire) and I stood between the fireplace and the sofa, which faced inwards and not towards the fireplace. All this I recall vividly. All Rene said rather casually was, he is not coming now and I don't want to talk about it. I didn't mention the subject but stayed on there until the next morning as though nothing had happened.

My own version of what happened was, a client of hers who had slept with her in the past phoned up for sex in the afternoon and was persistent when saying 'No' he would have said he was on his way calling at the flat. In the meantime she phoned me to tell me to say I was her fiancé. So when he came she told him her fiancé was on his way. He may have used some nasty words but did leave. This probably happened just before I arrived as to why she seemed dazed when I saw her.

I must have spent a great deal of time in the flat as I remember it so well. Space in a West End flat was at a premium so it was not a large flat. There were no landings so you walked into the front room when you entered. This part was quite large as it was a lounge and dining area. The other rooms at the end led straight into that room, they were small rooms. The bedroom contained a double bed, which took up most of the room. Perhaps I remember the bed as I spent some pleasant nights in it. again the bathroom was small but it had an unusual shaped bath more like a modern bath, again not much room. The kitchen and W.C I do not recall but they would have been tiny.

What else do I remember in the flat? Of course, this beautiful girl coming out of the bathroom in the nude to dry herself. There probably wasn't much room in the bathroom itself. I well remember her chiding me because I wouldn't do the same but I am shy in these matters and do not like walking about in the nude. My first wife Pat liked to walk around in the bedroom naked. Actually Pat said a strange thing when she was in the bath in Birstall Leicester. She thought the female figure was ugly. Of course I didn't agree but beauty is in the eye of the beholder.

One such memory is the signed photograph in a frame of Rene, which I had and Pat destroyed along with that of one of Aliki. While I know that I won a prize of Aliki's photo in a competition at the Dorchester. I cannot recall whether I had Rene done professionally or if she gave me one taken at one of her modelling sessions.

The everlasting vision of Rene will always be of her looking at me with those eyes and the pout of her lips when she wanted me to do something. I was like putty in her hands and would have done anything for her. This sums up everything I am sure of in my recollection apart from the final meeting. I can only rely on Dodie (my mother) and Neville Southwell to draw what happened between us, it is amazing that apart from seeing Rene in the flat and seeing the inside of the flat clearly in my mind I simply have no recollection as to where we went during those months. I cannot ever recall going to the Florida again during that time.

Dodie

I do know however and do well recall on three or four occasions I discussed Rene with Dodie. Dodie was well aware of my relationship with her so must have seen her fairly often. In fact Dodie must have liked her and probably thought at the time she would have been a better match for me than Pat.

The last conversation with Dodie about Rene is even clearer in my mind. My uncle Shirley's current girlfriend was called Jane and she was a close friend of my mother. I myself saw Jane sometime after the war probably 1946 or early 1947 when Dodie was in company with Jane and a number of other women. Jane was talking to the woman next to her and they were discussing a woman not present. My mother pricked up her ears when she heard the name Rene Thompson. She couldn't hear much of the conversation but Dodie told me when she saw me. I told her to ask Jane when she saw her next about Rene. I don't know whether she did or not but I didn't follow this up as I had other interests at the time.

I think this proves that Dodie knew Rene quite well as it is unlikely that she would have recalled the name Rene Thompson about seven years later.

Neville Southwell

A piece of luck here from one of his letters, I received this letter on the 5th April 1943 when I was stationed at Leicester. For some reason I must have been on leave and had visited Neville earlier in London.

Neville writes "How strange that you should have met Rene. I expect it did make you feel a little peculiar. After all you were pretty gay in those days and I think future generations will never know London night life as it was before the War. Rene wasn't really a bad little creature. I always rather liked her" I would point out that Rene was above normal height for a woman but Neville used the word 'little' a lot in his description.

I now come to the final meeting a memory, which has always stuck in my mind. I may not remember where I met Rene the day before but I certainly recall the day I saw her for the last time. I believe the flat she was living in was behind Marble Arch tube station and I had some difficulty in locating it like the first flat I can picture this one. It was on the ground floor and while I have been in many luxurious flats in my time this one was as equal to any. There was a vast room, which was the only room I saw with an imposing ornate fireplace with two large sofas either side.

I had tea with Rene and we talked a lot about the past but no romance at all, just a meeting between two old friends.

It has been an emotional time for me bringing back memories of a girl I must have been deeply in love with at the time and also such a sad emotion remembering so little of her compared to the other four.

They say that Authors fall in love with the heroines they create. Having written so much of Rene and so much of the gaps missing I can understand why. I think at the moment as an author I am falling into such a position. However I have so much else still to write that this will pass.

It is amazing that when one considers that a dance hostess whose living was to entertain men and whom I only knew for six months would be so excited seeing me again five years later and wish to show me the success she had become living in this opulent flat.

Was it her Patron who provided her flat or could it have been her Father? Jacqui found in her searches a similar name born in 1917, which was the year of Rene's birth. This Rene married in 1947 and died in 1949. Her Father was rich and died in 1946 leaving over half a million pounds (a vast sum in those days). He left the bulk to his son but the daughter only received £13,000. Had he provided for her in her lifetime to avoid then, what to him would have been an unacceptable vocation or did he express his disgust by leaving his daughter such a small amount in his Will? We will never know but if this Rene had red hair then quite probably it is one and the same.

I now say goodbye to this glamorous redhead and can only regret what might have been.

Chapter Eight

A Downward Trend

From the point I separated from Aliki until my marriage I did take a spiral dive, as I would be out in the West End at least five days in every week until 5am. Work naturally took a back seat. However the reader must be aware that during that period I did meet Rene whom I have already allotted a whole chapter to.

My life was tied to drink and women and will elaborate on some of these attractive species of the female race.

Diana was about twenty years old, attractive, tall with her hair always cut short. She was a very pleasant girl and even today when I hear the tune, 'I've Got You Under My Skin', I think of her. She was a hostess at The Coconut Grove club. At these clubs there was a system of booking hostesses for a session, rather like the way characters in a Jane Austin novel would reserve a dance, but in a slightly more basic way. I had booked her a few times but never ventured to her flat. One evening when I was with her I was struck with the idea of going down to the English Riviera; I imagined Torquay to be like Juan Les Pins. I asked her if she had ever been to Devon and she had not; I suspect she had never left London's bright lights, anyway she agreed on a week's holiday. When I called to collect her she said her friend Pat wished to come as well. I was a bit put out by this but there was nothing I could do so she came. First stop was Bournemouth's best hotel, The Royal Bath, where I booked a double for the girls, and a single for myself. Refined elderly ladies made up the bulk of the hotel's clientele and I will never forget the looks of horror as I took these brightly painted ladies into the lounge where all were having tea. The scene was straight from a Bateman cartoon. I kept a stiff upper lip but the girls could not have enjoyed the atmosphere more than I did. It was all too much for Diana and next day she got the train for London. Pat was more game and was happy to head for Devon. She came from Southend and had only been in London for a few weeks where Diana had taken her under her wing. I was therefore left with a girl strange to me for perhaps six days. This was not my plan. As we set off for Torquay our spirits lifted. Pat was young, blond and full of life. We chatted away and somehow I mentioned that I had never made love to a girl. She was most surprised saying she did not know such men existed and she indicated that she would soon rectify the situation, adding that she had lots of boyfriends, saying that they were her vocation. We booked a double room at The Palace, Torquay, the best hotel in town and after the first night I soon got the hang of things. Time was found for sightseeing. We went to the flea circus where the tiny creatures had miniature chariots tied to them and there were bets on who was going to win. In those days there were also frog jumping competitions. The frog with the greatest hop won. I recall Budweiser was the world champion. Pat did not want to return to London and asked me to drive her home to Southend, which I did. She was a sweet and loving girl and I had a vague notion at the time that I could temper her wayward ways. Twice later I visited her there but was not impressed by the town; my hotel was substandard and the place was full of day-trippers, candy-floss and rock. The redeeming feature was the pier, a mile long with a railway. Pat lived with her parents and her time was passed on the beach during the day and finding a boy to go out with in the evening. I really enjoyed her company and her libido was extraordinary; she was just a young girl wanting to enjoy herself, quite adorable and I wonder what happened to her. I hope she did not fall too far from grace.

I resumed my relationship with Diana for quite a few months where sex was always available at a price. When Rene came along I recommended an articled clerk friend of mine to her and if I recall correctly the offer was taken up.

Perhaps I may be allowed to say a word about the Ladies of the Night, a very ancient profession. The Restoration Aristocrats had their Courtesans and this was above board. The Victorians were no different except they kept everything hidden; their wives were for babies and their mistresses were for fun. I only strayed into this milieu for a period of a few weeks. This was in down-market clubs where the hostesses had just one thing in mind. There were in fact two levels of clubs; those like The Coconut Grove where the girls had their own flats and they would take the boys back if they liked them.

Then there were the disreputable places from which couples would go to shady lodgings in Paddington, where there were accommodating landladies. I remember one such landlady saying she did not usually allow men into her house, but as I was a gentleman who had been there before I was welcome – complete flannel! The personal hygiene of these girls was pas excellence. They went to great lengths to avoid those embarrassing diseases and I never came to grief.

Only once have I had my name in the tabloid press. I used to read The News of the World; it was a broadsheet in those days and the coverage of the sport was excellent. I enjoyed the scandals and never thought I would be included. Lillian, a hostess from The Paradise Club was the cause of my downfall. She was a blond from Wales, a year or two older than I and inclined to mother me!

We sat on the same table every evening and I would book her for the next day. She was affectionate but drew the line in actually making love. We got on well and she told me all about herself; she had a small son and hoped to make enough money to return to Wales with her husband to buy a house. I used to give her a lift home to Camden Town and one night when I was more drunk than usual I expected more than a few kisses for all the money I was spending. I followed her up the stairs and tried to go into the flat; there was a row, the husband came out and we had a fight. The Police arrived and then I found myself up in front of the Magistrate. 'An Englishman's home is his castle', he stated and this is what the Editor of The News of the World chose for his headline. That Magistrate could not have known Camden Town well. 'The Brecknock' was not quite Eaton Terrace. Once there were grand houses there but now they were let out as single rooms and many shady characters lived there. Ironically my grandmother grew up there in the areas heyday and just around the corner Dr Crippen had buried his wife in the garden.

After the publicity Lillian set off for the country and I did not see her for three weeks when we spent the evening together just to make things up. We parted on good terms and then Rene arrived on the scene. While I admire Lillian for her ambitions to save for her family's future I did not approve of her husband's role. The life of a nightclub hostess is a dangerous one and a husband should love his wife and care for her, which he did not. My last romance before matrimony involved Carol; an attractive lively blond who had a good job and a flat in Chelsea. She had been a girlfriend of my cousin Leslie and so must have liked Farmiloe's. She was different to all the other girls; she loved parties and was acceptable, almost, in High Society. The trouble was she was a tart. You could say 'one night stands' were her speciality. Money would not have changed hands but boyfriends had to be, if not big spenders, then medium-sized ones. I rashly contemplated marriage with Carol. Could I have tamed that minx? It would have been unwise to try. Neville had the last word. He reported that he had seen her after the war with a middle-aged American climbing into a large Buick outside Selfridges, running true to form.

Chapter Nine

Matrimony

Now I will tell the reader how I first encountered marriage, but first I must introduce The Tunnel Club. When you leave Belsize Park tube station there are houses to your left and to the right shops; and between the shops and the station there is an open space for a flower seller, which, is still there today. On the far side of the station are more shops and one of them was my gentleman's outfitter's business, trading under the name, Farmiloe Ltd. The flat where Dodie and I lived, in Holmfield Court, was just around the corner. The Tunnel Club and Howard's Restaurant were the first of these earlier shops. They shared an entrance and had separate doors and outside there was a cigarette machine belonging to the restaurant. When I was not down the West End The Tunnel Club, rather than the pubs further up the street, was my local. The club was run by an elderly couple, Hickie and his girlfriend, and they became very good friends of mine; they knew all the gossip, both local and from farther afield. I was a member of the Club for twenty years from 1936 to 1956. The entrance was through a long, thin passage and the premises were just as narrow inside. There were always plenty of people there and both my wives have been there a number of times. I knew everybody there and two stand out. There was a retired History Professor with whom I had great conversations with on history, and there was an Australian, Neil Bell, a good drinking companion, who wrote historical stories and also a book, which is worth reading, called Pinkney's Gardens about Southwold. After the war I called into the club in 1946 when, although not living in the vicinity, I was passing by. Most of the members were new except Hickie and his lady friend. One of the new members was a smartly-dressed Swedish lady, aged over fifty, and we had a few drinks. She invited me up to her flat, which was nearby, for a nightcap. It was beautifully furnished and I had just finished my drink and about to go when, to my surprise, she appeared from an adjoining room stark naked. She was a lot older than me, I was 31 at the time, and she was not my type. She saw my hesitation and added the doubtful inducement that she was too old to have a baby. I did not want to be rude and made a hurried exit, hoping at the same time that she would not catch cold.

Now back to October 1938. I did not feel like going up to the West End and, with supper inside me, decided on a few drinks in the Club. Then, at about 10 pm, deciding on an early night, I headed for home. By the entrance was a pretty waitress trying to get cigarettes for one of her customers from the machine. We got into friendly conversation and I said that if she gave me the money I would get a packet from the club. More banter followed and, enlivened by the drinks inside me, I asked for a date. She giggled and returned to the restaurant while I returned to The Tunnel Club for a further drink. Buoyed up I then went into the restaurant and, although not hungry, ordered a meal. All the girls were giggling and I found a table looked after by my girl. Goodness knows how much of the meal I ate and then I suggested to Pat, for that was her name, that we meet outside. I walked her home, twenty minutes up the hill, right at St. Stephen's Church where my parents were married and then down the hill past the Cinema and across the road to Constantine Road. Hampstead is a very smart area and this road was the boundary dividing the smart and the scruffy neighbourhoods. Kentish Town and Camden Town, although in the same postal area, were down market. I hoped to see her the next evening and planned a great hullabaloo if turned down. It was either on the following night or the next one that I proposed. Memory is a funny thing; the next fourteen days are a complete blank. We must have seen each other almost every day as we were making wedding arrangements. The void in my recollections is like the one with Rene. As those under twenty- one needed their parents or guardians permission all I can recall is Pat going down to the Isle of Wight to ask her aunt Alice for permission to marry.

Perhaps I should sketch out a little of Pat's background. She was born on 26th July 1919 and was about 5ft 7 tall with dark hair; she was attractive and outgoing. Little is known of her father, Mr Cotton, who could have had gypsy blood, as his daughter reflected that look. Nobody knows how long her parents were together but both died when Pat and her younger brother, Tommy, were little. Aunt Alice looked after them in Shanklin, Isle of Wight, although her father apparently came from Bristol. Pat came up to London, like many provincial girls at the age of 18, and lived in Constantine Road, Hampstead with a friend, Betty, and they pretended to be sisters. Well, as I recounted, we met in October 1938 and were married sixteen days later. We were divorced, the marriage a casualty of war, in 1945, the Decree Nisi coming through in March 1946. What went wrong? Looking back I blame myself as I was not really in love with her. She was just a very attractive, lively girl, but, with my track record, I was not ready for marriage. When I realised I was deeply in love with her it was too late. She certainly was in love with me from the start; as she had never met anyone before of my social background, who was well off and had experience of High Society. But our dreams gradually faded and she became cynical, hard and, I am afraid miserable. After me followed four husbands in the United States, although one was a bigamist. Sadly she never found happiness again; there was a short time with Richard, her second husband, with whom she had two sons, but there was too much 'emotional baggage' and Richard found her in bed with another man, and that was that.

Our wedding must have been one of the strangest of all times. Dodie, whom I telephoned a few days before, was the only member of my family to know what I was up to. She was now living alone in a cottage in Kirby Cross, near Frinton-on-Sea. She had been in love with Freddie Brigdon, who lived with his wife in Frinton. Freddie's was an unhappy marriage and the love of Dodie and Freddie lasted for thirty years until he died. He was actually a very nice man.

My first witness was Frank L'Estrange Heppard, whose father was a dentist in Blackburn. He was an Old Uppinghamian but our paths did not cross at school, as he was a few years older than I. The middle name, L'Estrange, struck me as indicating some mysterious antecedents. Frank had curly brown hair, and, with a hump back, looked slightly distinguished. We had bumped into each other in the West End and from the Uppingham bond a friendship developed. Later Frank and I got involved with a conman, named Smith. This rogue was about sixty years old, charming, pleasant and good company. Two young inexperienced gentlemen were a gift to him. Frank had known Smith for about six months and then began doing business with him. Things were getting nasty between them when I became involved; Smith alleged that Frank owed him money and I happily bailed him out. I now have the benefit of all the documents. I find I invested £100 in a company called London and Provincial Marketing Agencies Ltd. It ceased trading after six months and shortly afterwards was struck off the register. I also loaned £175 to Frank; so I laid out £275 in all, £13,340 in today's money.

The two witnesses, Frank and Jenny, another waitress from the restaurant, and Pat and I all met up at St. Pancreas Registry Office. Little did I know that nine years later I would wed again in the same place, and again the ring would be bought from Bravington's in Kings Cross. I never saw either of the witnesses again although I did try and contact Frank at the AA where he made his career. Once the ceremony was over we all went in separate directions. Pat with Jenny back to Howard's Restaurant where they were short staffed and they did not want to let them down. Frank and I had a long chat and he gave me some friendly advice; remember I knew little about how women worked. I may have had plenty of girlfriends but my knowledge of the gentler sex was small. I knew nothing of their inner workings.

For the first night of our honeymoon I arranged to meet Pat at midnight at a guest house in Kensington. I should have booked a room at a good hotel, I could afford it, and perhaps I did not think she was ready for anything so grand. The guest house turned out to be a disaster. It was run by two young men who were cheerful and pleasant enough but when we arrived they announced that they had overbooked. There was a double bed in a large room available but there was a single bed there as well occupied by a young woman of about thirty. She was however pleasant enough and told us not to worry about her being there. The bathroom was down the corridor, anyhow I was fortified with a few drinks, my bride was sober and we survived the night. Looking back it must have been one of the most unromantic wedding nights of all time; we were strangers to each other and had yet to be really committed.

The next day was an improvement; it could not anyway have been worse. Even then there was a bad start. I announced that Dodie always sat in the front of my Jag and so Pat would have to sit in the back, this made my new bride rightly indignant. All this shows how unprepared I was for marriage and Pat, no doubt, wondered what she had done to deserve such treatment. Things perked up when we arrived at Dodie's cottage at Kirby Cross and, unlike her reaction to Dorothy, my second wife, she was very welcoming to Pat. Years later, after my divorce, she was to stay with her in America. In contrast my grandmother never liked Pat and thought Dorothy a better match for her grandson.

In the evening we drove to the local pub to meet Freddie Brigdon and that night all was consummated. Many years later Dorothy was to sneer at me saying how did I know Pat was a virgin and how lucky I was to deflower a nineteen-year-old. 'Did you break her cherry?' was the expression she used. I do not wish to run Dorothy down, she truly loved me but she was eaten up by the 'the green eyed monster'. Of my two wives, one was unfaithful and the other jealous. I do not know which caused me most misery.

On the third day we drove back to Hampstead, as I had rented a house in Willow Walk overlooking the Heath. Like the other houses in Willow Walk it had character, with a nice garden, back and front; the furnishings were good and it was our home for three months. Today the rent of such a house would be £10,000 a month.

On the fourth day of the honeymoon we stayed in bed all day making love over and over again - breaking off only for a well earned cup of tea. Pat was highly sexed, far more than I. The first year we were together was something I have never experienced since. Perhaps if the war had not intervened our marriage would have survived. There was never such passion in my second marriage, but then Dorothy and I were more mature and past the first flush of youth. Anyhow by the evening of the fourth day we were quite hungry and the larder being empty we set off to The Continental for supper. The next few weeks were spent around Hampstead, either in The Continental or The Tunnel Club. Also we ventured up to the West End to visit cinemas and old haunts like The White Monkey Club.

The Continental was run by three Italian brothers. Gus the eldest had left before I first went there and the second brother and his wife seemed to be in charge (Chez and his Italian wife Marie). The youngest brother Freddie Moruzzi had a Scottish wife called Jean. Chez was interned for part of the war but Freddie was not. Actually both Freddie and Jean were clients of mine for over thirty years

When the lease of Willow Road ran out we moved into 63 Upper Park Road, a house near Belsize Park. My shop and The Tunnel Club were conveniently nearby and The Continental only about a quarter of an hour's walk away. The house had two stories and a large attic, which made the marital bedroom. There was a small front garden and most of the back garden was made up of a double garage. We put a lot of effort into furnishing the home but we had to give it up in June 1939 when I went bankrupt. As well as the furniture we purchased a number of pedigree dogs, all puppies, and the double garage was used as a kennel and the car parked in the road. Budgie, my grandmother, then living in Suffolk, asked her sister, great aunt May, to call. This she did and when I opened the garage door all the puppies rushed out. The report went back to Suffolk that we were quite mad. May should have taken all this in her stride; she herself had a Pekinese called Chichi Boo and when he died she bought another Pekinese and named him Boo Two.

Pat had a seventeen-year-old younger brother called Tommy. Up until then I had not met him and we said he could come and stay, so he set off on his first train journey to London. We had a Swedish au pair but Tommy's hormones were rather active and she had to leave. My only other recollection of this house concerned a splinter I got stuck in my hand. I am squeamish so Pat and Tommy sat on top of me while Pat removed the offending object.

It was late 1938 or early 1939 that I first went down in the Jag to the Isle of Wight. Even if you are going by train Shanklin is easy to get to. It is an attractive small town with one main street and the famous Chimes leading down to the beach. Pat's aunt Alice lived there in a small cottage in a cul-de-sac called Orchardleigh. The dwellings were very old fashioned and I suspect they have now been demolished. Aunt Alice's cottage was the last one, No 16. The four rooms were tiny, two up, two down with a steep staircase. The first time I visited auntie in Shanklin Pat was so worried of what I would think, as the house was so different to what I was used to. She needn't have worried a I became very fond of auntie. Pat and I had the room to the right, which had just enough room for a double bed. Our daughter, Susan, was born in this room on 14th February 1944, Pat and I decided to call our daughter after my grandmother. As Budgie's name was Fanny this caused some merriment, so we decided to use Budgie's second name, which was Elizabeth. Hence our daughter became Susan Elizabeth Farmiloe. On the ground floor was a front parlour containing the good furniture; this room was never used when I was there. Aunt Alice slept, cooked and ate in the rear room and there was an outside loo.

Aunt Alice was confined to an armchair in the kitchen for the last ten years. In fact she slept in the chair as she suffered from terrible ulcers on her legs and the bandages had to be continually changed. On one occasion Pat and I were able to get her into the Jag and drove her right round the Island, she appreciated this gesture very much.

Aunt Alice's surname was Ford and she was the eldest of four sisters; she had broken the golden rule and had a baby out of wedlock. This baby was Lene, then she was about forty years old and she must have played a large part in bringing up Pat and Tommy. She had a job as a cook to Dr Melhuish in Shanklin. Her life must have been hard; she had her mother Alice, the two children (Pat & Tommy) and a full-time job on her hands. She did finally marry and I hope she found happiness.

Aunt Alice had three sisters, Pat's mother, one in South Africa, and, the most interesting one, Nellie. She had a domineering character and was feared by everyone else. I have a letter, dated 18 January 1946 from Tommy's wife, Linda in which she said she had heard from aunt Nellie who was as two-faced as ever and she added that she detested people like that but as long as she left her alone she would be alright. Nellie lived in Winchester with uncle Will where she ran a sweet shop. No shop girl lasted long as she could not trust them. When Pat was seventeen she stayed there for a while and there was a job lined up for her in a Departmental Store, then Lene rescued her sending her 10/- for the fare home. I have a typical Nellie letter, which she sent after my divorce in February 1948. She wrote, 'I have prayed to God to send me news of my niece Pat. Lene has written to me to saying that she has left Shanklin without saying Goodbye. I am sure Lene stirred up trouble between you two and that she drove Pat away.' How stupid are family rows and how small-minded people can become. We are given our relatives but at least we can choose our friends.

Pat and I once motored down to see Nellie and Will in Winchester. Will was pompous and had done rather well for himself. He was a Labour Councillor in Winchester where there could not have been many of his party. But of course he was as conservative as the next man, always immaculately dressed in a dark suit and white collar. Nellie was proud of his position and rammed this fact down the throats of the rest of the family and anyone else who would listen. But to give this couple their due they gave Pat and I a warm welcome. I was on my best behaviour and I hope they thought their niece had made a good choice.

It was a great year for me the first year of our marriage. I was married to somebody who relied on me a great deal. Pat was new to the big city and I showed her a life, which was entirely new to her. We were inseparable and I vividly recall a friend being surprised that even when Pat went to the toilette I had to hold her hand. We were so much in love.

I have not been back to the Isle of Wight since 1947 but I recall the Island has a lot to offer. Godshill is one of the prettiest villages I have ever seen. Then there is the yachting at Cowes, Carisbrooke Castle, Alum Bay, The Needles and quaint Ventnor. Perhaps one day I will go back with my daughter Susan and revisit the place she was born.

I have mentioned my menswear shop and now perhaps I can give a few more details about it. When, at the age of twenty- one I received my inheritance, I gave up my articles with the Chartered Accountants, Jocelyn, Miles and Page and I invested in a shop. This choice was a good one. I had an excellent manager, Johnson and the location, on the ground floor of a block of flats, Gilling Court, opposite Belsize Park Tube, was sound and I lived with my mother, Dodie, in a flat around the corner. I decided to go in for high class men's wear. There was no nearby competition and it was an affluent area. My nearest rival, Moody's, now no longer, was two miles away in the Finchley Road. There were other shops in Hampstead but they were another mile away. Johnson was very experienced and he could dress a window. We sold only the best and dealt with all dress-wear, accessories, evening dress-suits, white bow ties; we sold silk ties at 6/6d and cheaper ones at 1/6d. There were the best Wolsey socks as well as some expensive ones from Two Staples. Also we had sports coats and expensive flannels called Daks, from Simpson's at one guinea. The hats came from Dunn and Falcon and gloves from Dents and Fownes. Our most popular shirts were Van Housen at 10/6. We also stocked Viyella and Clydella from Hollins who are still going today. Everyone then wore a hat and we had bowlers and trilby's as well as rolled umbrellas. In fact we sold everything except suits.

We advertised in the tube lift in Belsize Park. I was proud of these posters and we claimed to provide for Britons from the Stone Age, through Medieval times, the Restoration, the Dandies of the Regency and Georgian England. Our slogan was 'Fitted up by Farmiloe's'. The shop itself was a fair size with windows on either side of the door, on the left were modern glass shelves and in front were glass display cabinets which left plenty of space for serving. We had office space at the back of the shop. Johnson's wages were 45/- a week and we employed a junior aged about seventeen. I enjoyed helping out when I felt like it and was a dab hand at tying ties for customers. We once had a heavily-built well-spoken customer who bought half-a-dozen sets of expensive underwear and insisted on trying them on and taking the junior with him into the changing room, which was in the basement of the shop. Then he came in for another six sets and repeated the process. Johnson spotted that he was a pervert and put a stop to him.

I owned a second shop in Cricklewood High Street, which I bought as a going concern. The area was a bit run down but the business had been going for a number of years. Most of the clothes were sold on tic using a card system backed by a firm called The Provident, which incidentally was owned by a Mr Waddilove, whose son was an Old Uppinghamian. While Johnson was an overall manager there was Humphries who ran my branch shop. He was a nice chap and walked with a limp, following a football accident. He had been to school with Denis and Leslie Compton. Humphries was paid 30/- a week. Johnson and I looked for further sites for expansion, including Colindale and Edgeware but we could not find a suitable building. Things started to go wrong when Johnson was offered a better position by a firm called Morgan and Balls in the Strand. I advertised for a new manager and, as there was a lot of unemployment at the time, I had a huge response. Applicants were required to call at the shop and about fifty turned up queuing down the street.

My maternal grandfather helped me interview but he was no use as he kept talking about clothes when he was a young man such as spats. We reduced the applicants to a short list of about ten. Then suddenly Johnson reappeared saying he missed working for me and that he wanted to come back, but Morgan and Balls upped his salary and he was away again. By then I had dismissed all the earlier applicants and not kept the notes on them so the whole process had to be repeated. This time only a dozen turned up and they were no good. The one I eventually chose was to be paid on a commission basis. He and his wife were about ten years older than Pat and I and he became very patronising and too friendly. We ended going out as an unsatisfactory foursome. He wanted a quick turnover and bought job lots with a view to selling stock quickly and this is not what the clientele of Belsize Park wanted; Camden Town perhaps, but not Belsize Park; trade deteriorated and eventually we went bust. After the war I met up with Johnson who had been in the RAF and had now decided to become a teacher; we had tea together and he insisted on paying, a turnaround from the old days. My lifestyle came to an end when I went bankrupt.

I have a file on the bankruptcy. I paid myself £4 a week, the cost of a night out at The Dorchester with Aliki. Farmiloe Ltd had a nominal capital of £1,000, divided into £1 shares. Both Fred Tordoff and I put £500 into the business and it was declared bankrupt on 15 July 1939 owing me £1,300, a Director's loan. I received only 1/- in the pound dividend, but I had guaranteed the creditors and so owed £1,430. It was not the greatest of business ventures. Fred played no part in the running of the business and lost his £500. He was very decent about it. I asked Jocelyn, Miles and Page to arrange the winding up of Farmiloe Ltd. They sent along Charles Barrett, who I knew well to do the job. Then followed my own bankruptcy; uncle Shirley found a solicitor, who in fact was a crook and later went to prison for using client's money. He was a charming man, as I suspect most financial crooks are. He firstly advised me to resign from the Artist's Rifles, my TA Regiment. If I had stayed I would have got a Commission in the war, gone into the Infantry and most likely been killed. The first to go was my beloved Jag, which went for a song. Had I been able to keep it and stored it at Henstead it would have been worth a fortune after the war. Here are listed the key dates and amounts. –

Statement of Affairs Submitted	11.8.1939
Adjudged Bankrupt	18.10.1939
Discharged from Bankruptcy	20.3.1945

Statement of Affairs Submitted

Call on Guarantees on behalf of Farmiloe Ltd	1,457.9.4
Due on Furniture, Rent and Household Stores	227.3.9
Overdrafts and Loans	284.16.11
Garage Charge	59.15.2
Telephone, Gas, Electricity and Water	42.5.6

Clothes	27.2.0
Sundries	25.14.10
	£2104.7.6
Assets realised – Listed as £134.11.9	98.18.00
Deficit	£2,005.9.6

The Registrar went on to say that I was educated at a well-known Public School and then Articled to a firm of Chartered Accountants from 1934 to 1936. Then he listed my inheritance and continued, 'In the meantime the Bankrupt was leading an extravagant and, it would seem, dissipated life, spending money freely on entertaining, drinking and nightclubs. Further in 1937 he lost £784 speculating on the Stock Exchange, and he spent £70 on a three week tour of the Continent and lost £200 on betting on racehorses. He added that I was a candid and straightforward witness and that I made no attempt to conceal the fact that my downfall was due to extravagance. Finally he stated that my lifestyle hindered my ability to run my company properly. I do not argue with all this. I was now penniless but Budgie came to my rescue and sent me a monthly allowance. This was a great help and, while cutting out white ladies, we were able to live adequately. This allowance went on for ten years, which is just as well as I could never have survived on my Army pay. It only stopped when Dorothy insisted I give it up, which put her high in Budgie's estimation. Pat was terrific after I went bust and never reproached me for it. A great comfort, she just buckled down and got on with things.

We rented a small flat in a back street of Camden Town for just one week; moving on because the area was too rough. I recall going down to the newsagents to buy a Sunday paper and wondering how all this happened and how lucky I was to have Pat. Our next stop was in the country, the village of Boxmore in Hertfordshire. We were an hour's train journey from town and lived in a cottage in Feather Bed Lane. All was pleasant and peaceful and we made friends with the farmer next door. In town I had a collection of about two hundred 78 rpm gramophone records but I only managed to transport about a third of them, which I still have, and I never returned for the rest.

Our wedding had been in October and with all the passionate lovemaking it was no surprise that Pat was pregnant and, as the baby was due in August, we decided to return to town and we found a nice flat overlooking Regent's Park. The day before Michael was born we went to the new and luxurious Gaumont Palace Cinema in Camden. I cannot remember the film but between the A and the B showing there was a stage act by Donald Piers, then a newcomer but after the war a big star. His song was, If I knew you were coming I would bake a cake. George Michael Farmiloe was born the next day, August 26th 1939. We took a taxi to the hospital in Holloway. I returned at 3am in the morning and walking home was stopped by a Policeman who asked what was in the bag, 'Ladies clothes' I replied and then I explained that my wife had just given birth. We all knew that the war was about to break out so, anticipating that London was about to be bombed, we left town. No one anticipated eight months of phoney war.

So Pat, myself, Michael, Otto, the Dachshund and two Chows embarked to Shanklin . We must have been driven down there by Neville Southwell as a letter from him states 'I shall always remember our journey on the first day of war. I had two brainless ideas to earn some money. Firstly there was a job in Portsmouth serving in a Naval outfitters. I had the experience and, as well, had to stay in digs, but being a shop assistant for someone else after having one's own shop was difficult. I lasted just one week. The next crazy scheme was to work as a door-to-door salesman. I bought some commodities from a wholesaler and tried to sell them at people's homes. In all I only managed to sell two items and then I called it a day. Then I joined up, and with Pat's child allowance from the Army, the 1/- a day Army pay and the money from Budgie we were able to get a flat over a shop in Shanklin High Street; a step in the right direction.

CHAPTER TEN

Army Days

I joined the Army on 17th April 1940 and my record card described me as follows: height 5ft 8 1/2 inches, weight 147 lbs, chest 37 inches, complexion pale, eyes brown, hair brown and distinctive marks, scar on right knee. (This was acquired while riding my tricycle at Avening House). I am still about the same but the hair has gone. I was discharged on 2nd February 1946. They said of me, 'conduct good, intelligence above average and a quick and conscientious worker. He shows a rapid grasp of all situations arising from his duties'. My army life was not dull; in fact it was very eventful. I started as a private and finished as such and for the whole war I did not leave British shores, but life for Private 7669315 Farmiloe was lively. I did in fact, with some trepidation, volunteer before my call-up date as I expected a commission, which I would have had had I stayed in the Artist's Rifles. Anyhow I was twenty-five when I joined up and had no problem mixing with people from totally different backgrounds. England then was a country with many class divisions, but in spite of my background I made numerous friends, many of whom I kept in touch with for many years after the war. I am both interested in and fond of my fellow man and the army taught me a lot about friendship. I now consider myself classless and, as the old saying goes, I can mix with both Smith and Lord Rosebery.

I was ordered to report, with the help of a free pass, to Hilsea Barracks, Cosham, Portsmouth, the home of one of the Army Pay Corps, on April 17th 1940, which, via the ferry, was a short journey from Shanklin. I was to serve in six of these offices around the country and none, in my time, were bombed. In due course, with two hundred other soldiers, I was placed in a large room behind a desk; we were divided into sections, each under an Officer. Mine was Captain Booth, goodness knows where he came from, perhaps he was a soldier from the first war, but he was well past his sell-by date. We were shortly to cross swords; he was full of his own self importance and at once complained when I did not call him, 'Sir'. The days were enlivened by Private Butcher who periodically had an epileptic fit, which was both chilling and frightening. To talk to he was a very nice chap and I hope he was soon discharged, as he was not fit to serve. Then we were issued with gas masks and for an hour a day we wore them when working. They were not too uncomfortable, but working in them was difficult; no one thought gas would be used and I doubted the masks' effectiveness but no doubt they boosted civilian morale. I recall on one occasion the Commanding Officer paraded the whole corps, about five hundred officers and men, and complained about our adding up. In those days, of course, there were no adding machines. He gave us all a mental arithmetic question and as this was just up my street I shot my hand up with the correct answer. Everyone was surprised but no promotion followed. Besides Butcher the only other fellow soldier I recall from this time, and who became a friend, was Private McIsaacs who was shortly to leave and gain a Commission. None of us slept in barracks and we all had to find digs. I had a good run of landladies who looked after me and treated me like a son. Often at weekends I could get leave and would make for the Isle of Wight where Pat, Michael and the dogs were living in the flat in Shanklin High Street.

Only one member of my family was killed in the War, Captain Robin Farmiloe, who was killed at Dunkirk. He was the son of great uncle Arthur and great aunt Connie who lived nearby in Hampstead. Robin was two years older than I and I last saw him in 1938 when great aunt Alice gave a cocktail party in her flat in Frognal. Robin's widow, Esther, who remarried, used to come to the Farmiloe reunions in the 1960s.

The first seven months of conflict were the 'phoney war' and those on the mainland did not feel any effect until Dunkirk, when the Germans started bombing the coastal towns, Portsmouth being one of the first. I recall one evening with colleagues watching their bombers flying over Cosham and then turning over the hills at the back and dropping their payload on Portsmouth. There were no British planes around so the enemy had a clear run. The Battle of Britain was in September 1940 and just before this I was transferred to the Knightsbridge Pay Office where I was in time for the Blitz. It was good to be back in London, my hometown. I had been away a whole year and, at first, the Germans were quiet and life was undisturbed. On the same posting was Staff Sergeant Blundell, I have forgotten his Christian name, and although different ranks we teamed up. He was about twenty-four and this was his first time in London. I showed him around town, which was quite an adventure for him and also introduced him to Carol (whom you will recall Neville Southwell mentioned in one of his letters getting into a Buick outside Selfridges). We would catch the tube to the West End; the stations were crowded with people who were living underground. To get off a train one stepped over sleeping bodies and the smell was awful. Blundell was keen to get on in life. He had joined the army before the war and wished to apply for a commission. Once, with his education, this would have been difficult but now there was a great shake-out and I hope he achieved his goal. He was keen on work, culture and a lively social life. I never discovered what happened to him.

While stationed in town I called on Neville who was working at the Brompton Hospital. He was kept busy with all the air raid victims and I stayed a night there chatting with the young doctors. I always thought that so many patients passed through their hands that they were immune to emotional and physical involvement. But this was not the case; people in chocolate factories may get fed up with chocolate, but these doctors were forever fascinated by the curves and winks of the young female body.

Unless you experienced the Blitz it is hard to imagine it and as a Londoner I am proud to have lived through it. At first it was just coastal towns that experienced the bombing; London was not prepared and it was hoped the anti-aircraft balloons would protect us, but they were useless and only fighter planes, which were in short supply, were effective. Anti-aircraft guns would charge up and down the streets; they were not very effective but were good for morale. Towards the end of the war when V1s and V2s came these guns were more use. With the flying bombs you were safe as long as you could hear the drone, but once the engine cut off you knew it was about to land.

The atmosphere in London during the blitz has never been repeated before or since. Each morning when you went out you witnessed whole rows of houses bombed-out and streets full of rubble. Everyone talked to one another from the highest to the lowest. Tragedy made every one equal and life went on as usual. There were air raid shelters for cover at night and each house had an Anderson corrugated iron shelter dug into the garden. At nightfall whole families would squeeze into them, stocking up with food and toys. My shelter was quite social; I met a nice girl at a party but, now, a married man, I behaved myself. She suggested that her father, a Colonel Wallace, the chief ARP warden for the district, could arrange shelter for me in the basement of a large block in Knightsbridge. There were about forty of us down there and with the various luxuries that we acquired it was like a select nightclub. Once the Colonel asked me to join him on the roof of the flats to witness a spectacle I hope I never see again. The enemy had set the city alight with firebombs. It was an awesome sight; the inhabitants had nowhere to go and the conflagration must have been worse than the Great Fire of 1666. In retrospect the bombing was not as bad as the carpet bombing of Dresden or Hamburg carried out by the Allies at the end of the war, let alone the devastation caused by the Atomic Bombs dropped on Japan. I recall one night in November 1940 when there was no bombing. We all experienced a great sense of relief until we discovered that the Germans had flattened Coventry. In our shelter everyone slept on mattresses, which were spaced close to one other. My next door neighbour was Princess Indira from India, who was in her early thirties and very attractive. She worked for the BBC World Service as a Broadcaster. We got on well but all was platonic. She slept on her left side and I on my right. 'Goodnight Douglas', she would say. 'Goodnight Indira', I would say. We were so close I could have kissed her, but I did not. Little did I know that back in Shanklin, Isle of Wight, Pat, my wife was finding comfort in the arms of Lance Corporal Green. Jay was born nine months later in August 1941.

The army decided I was due for a more active life than pen pushing and all those who were A1 fit were transferred to Aldershot. This is a town totally dominated by the army and after a few days of drilling I was interviewed by a panel of officers to see if I had officer potential. There were two key questions – 'What school did you go to?' The answer, 'Uppingham', was clearly a pass, and, secondly, 'Do you have a bank account?' Although an undischarged bankrupt I could reply, 'Yes', as, for some unknown reason, Lloyds Bank had never closed my account and, although the account was dormant, I had recently received a statement. Anyway I was one of twelve who passed the tests and then we were stranded in Aldershot with nothing to do, no parades, no drill, just allowed to idle. I made two friends, the first was private Harding who was about forty and had been a Captain in the Indian army, but this did not count for the home service. He found it very difficult taking orders from NCOs. My other companion was black. Blacks were uncommon. I had met Sam and the other entertainers in The Nest club, but I had not got to know them well, but this fellow was public school educated and a Chief in his own country and was one of the most charming and interesting people I had ever met.

My next posting was High Leigh, a small camp a few miles from Warrington, where I spent four weeks. For one of these I had my arm in a sling. We were doing a training exercise where one had to cross a small river on a rope attached each end to trees. I cleared the river, but let go too early and hit the bank. We also had a lot of drilling; sergeants still barked the orders but now they were dealing with officer cadets and I was addressed as Cadet Farmiloe. We also took turns to command the drilling. I was not good at this but fortunately the NCOs gave most of the commands. Other time was taken up with lectures on the theory and art of war. Great opportunities were provided for the ordinary soldier and NCO in wartime. In peacetime he would retire as a RSM but now things were different, many of them were commissioned, becoming Captains straight away.

While at High Leigh Pat wrote to me to say she was expecting a baby and that Terry Green was the father. I had to do something to save my marriage and explained the circumstances to my commanding officer. He did not want me to leave but allowed my return to the pay corps where I could be reunited with Pat in lodgings, and I was given a week's compassionate leave. I set off for the Isle of Wight and Pat met me at the station. I am short sighted and do not usually wear glasses when out and about as I can see distances without them. So in fact I walked straight passed Pat, who was wearing plenty of make-up, and her friend, who were both waiting. 'Isn't that your husband?' asked the friend. Anyhow we went back to the flat and had an unholy row. In those days I had a short temper and smashed a favourite ornament. Pat gave me another to destroy and I calmed down. I demanded that she choose between Terry Green, and our son Michael and me. She was not prepared to abandon Michael and so Terry was to go and she decided to go to Okehampton, where he was stationed, and tell him everything was over. I agreed to this on the condition that she left the Isle of Wight and joined me at my new posting in Leeds.

Terry Green was from Birmingham. He was serious-minded and rather moody, wrote poetry and smoked a pipe. In 1938 he had spent a holiday in Shanklin and there had been a holiday romance between him and Pat. He returned in 1939 but Pat was in London with me. He was back again in 1940 when I was stationed in Portsmouth and then the affair took off. Pat kept her word and Terry was no longer a threat. Jay was born on 14 August 1941 in Leicester and I brought him up as though he was my own. Magnanimously I invited Terry to Leicester one weekend, for a one and only time, to see his offspring. The visit, surprisingly, was quite civilized.

Pat was a great letter writer, writing well with excellent handwriting and every day, while in the Army, I received long interesting letters. This kept up while she was with Terry and also, later, when she was with her next lover, Richard. After Leeds, we lived together for two and a half years in Leicester and had we been able to stay there we would not have separated and divorced. The letters continued when she went to America and married Richard when they contained news of Susan, my daughter. In 1953 Dorothy, by kicking up a big fuss, stopped them and destroyed every single letter I had ever received, well over two hundred. I still have a marvellous collection of letters, over one hundred from Budgie, but not one from Pat. I do have one fragment of her writing, on the back of a picture of Susan on her twenty-first birthday. It states, 'Your little girl, now a woman'.

I knew Leeds a little as I had spent six weeks there as an articled clerk in 1935. My soldier's pay was 1/- a day so there were no dinners at Hagen Bach or rooms at The Metropole. My stay there lasted four months and the Church Parades stick out in my memory. Nostalgically I returned to Marshall and Snellgrove to visit their lifts, but my lift-girl of seven years earlier was not to be found. Perhaps I could include a letter here from one of my Army friends, which illustrates Army life and how we communicated.

7674023 Gunner Barrett

RHQ 80th (SH) Medium Ret RA

C/O GPO Norwich

18.1.1943

Dear Doug

I was glad to get your letter but I'm afraid I'm not very prompt again in replying. As you will see my address is again different and I'm am now reposing in East Anglia. The SH stands for Scottish Horse and as you may guess I am now forced to wear a bonnet with red pom-pom on it. Do I look cute! The Regiment comes from Perthshire and is the sort of pet Regiment of the Duke of Atholl and has the same headgear as worn on his Estate. I managed to get ten days leave after all from December 1st and was expecting to spend another Christmas away from home. We had only been back from leave four days when we were told that three fellows were wanted for this unit. I and two of my pals volunteered and when we arrived we were told we were going on eleven days leave from the following Monday. So I was home for Xmas and the New Year. It is a very good unit and we have settled down well.

Norwich is a fine place and has far more entertainment than any other town I've encountered so far. There are dances every night at some place or other and I don't know how all the cinemas manage to stay open, but they all seem to do well. There is a magnificent Cathedral and we went voluntarily to a service there last Sunday morning. The service was too High Church for me.

Yours

Frank

I recall thinking that it must have been a worry for Frank's mother for, beside himself, he had a brother in India and another in the Navy. I wonder if they all survived.

From June 1941 I spent two and a half years based in Leicester and they were the best years of my Army life. They were good years firstly because married life with Pat was working well; we were in love with each other, there was little money but that did not hinder us. On one occasion we did decide to take precautions. Pat purchased a box of Rendalls. The idea was to place one in the vagina and allow ten minutes to elapse before you went through the sexual act. I well recall this when Pat in her nudity carried out the instructions on the packet. I was in bed waiting for Pat to join me and there was Pat walking in the nude waiting for the ten minutes to elapse before getting into bed. There was I waiting almost dozing off and losing my urge. The packet finished up in the dustbin the next morning. It was quite an amazing occasion, which we never forgot.

The Leicester office housed a large Pay Corps and we were based in two converted warehouses, and we catered for the Royal Artillery. My section covered the Light Artillery, the Light Ack-Ack. Pat and I rented a house in the attractive village of Birstall, about six miles from the city. We were in the High Street next door to the greengrocer's shop. The owners of the shop also owned the house I was renting and was run by a very nice middle-aged couple. The woman had red hair and a very large mouth but was always very kind to us and also babysat for us. The only problem was she kept mixing my name up with my son Michael and she used to tell the neighbours what a lovely sight it was seeing Douglas playing about in the garden naked. There was a pub down the High Street, which, babysitters allowing, we visited on occasions and for a while we had two lodgers from the Pay Corps, Lillington and Jones.

I would catch the bus into Leicester each morning and on Friday nights I would go drinking with my pals, making sure I caught the last bus home at 10pm. One evening I drank too much, missed the bus and had to walk home. On reaching the village I lost my rucksack with papers in it, but the village policeman, who knew everyone, returned it to me the next day. He had seen me swinging the sack around and it had suddenly landed in someone's garden. Occasionally there were Army dances. Pat was easily the most attractive girl there and once an Officer took a fancy to her, creating a problem, as I could not tell him to clear off. One soldier said "Cor blimey fancy Farmiloe having a corker of a wife" I was always very proud when walking out with her.

I had a stroke of luck when my great uncle Lewis left me £200 in his will. This was about £9,000 in today's money. The only investment I made with these funds was in a tennis racquet, otherwise we blew the lot. One evening, taking a taxi there and back, we had an expensive dinner at The Grand Hotel in Leicester. Pat looked fantastic in her evening dress and it was just like the old days. I was not normally allowed to wear civilian clothes but I did on this occasion. There were several officers in the hotel who recognised me but I remained unchallenged.

I was often on picket duty, which involved guarding our building at night, and the next day we had off. There were a dozen of us positioned on the top floor and we took it in turns to walk around the perimeter. Basically we were watching out for fires, as break-ins were unlikely. Sleeping was not allowed and we passed the time writing letters, reading and playing cards. One of my correspondents, Jack Andrews, lived with his wife, Dorothy and daughter, Madeline in Perivale, Middlesex. After the war Dorothy, my second wife, and I would visit them and I recall going to a dance held by his employees, Macfarlane Lang at The Biscuit Inn. I mentioned to Jack that my divorce from Pat was taking a long time coming through. His father worked at the Divorce Courts in the Strand and he kindly put my file on the top of the pile. Things moved quickly after that.

I was transferred to the Royal Army Service Corps in October 1943. We had to give up the home in Birstall where we had a lodger, Kay, who was a bus conductress. I did not like her but she got on well with Pat. I did however like a friend of Pat's who came to stay for about six months. She had been the year earlier Beauty Queen of Shanklin. The attractive blond got on well perhaps some may say too well. One evening when Pat had gone to bed early Jean and I were on the sofa and this led to kissing and cuddling but nothing further. Pat came downstairs and we ended up on the wrong side of my wife.

However the incident was soon forgotten but my wife didn't in future go to bed before me. At the time of the move Pat was expecting Susan and the first thing she did was to farm out Michael. I never met the family but the arrangement was disastrous and we later found out that, while there, he was sexually abused. There was a curious incident when he was chased around the garden by the foster father who fell into a large hole, injuring himself. The man was furious with him and punished him. Being only four at the time he was rather hazy in his recollections of all this and at first they were incorrectly accounted to Mr and Mrs Booth, his next foster parents. Uncle Shirley took intervening action and he was moved to the Booths who lived in Robertsbridge in Sussex. They were ideal. They had no children of their own, but one adopted daughter. Mrs Booth was a nurse and they fostered seven other children of various ages. They lived in a house with a large garden and came with the highest recommendations. Michael was to stay for two years. Jay was found a place near Leicester where the carer complained that he had been left with hardly any clothes. Pat was furious and removed him and off he went with her and Kay.

In November 1943 I was transferred to Bury St Edmunds and from there I got a weekend pass to visit Pat. I had not seen her for six weeks and she was living in a wooden house on a hill with a fenced garden in Wiltshire. There was another girl there who I had not seen before. Jay must have been staying in the Isle of Wight. There was a romance going on at this time between her and a young Welsh officer. When I arrived I found her attitude to me totally changed. I wanted to spend the time available with her but she insisted in setting off to the pub with the housemate. We had plenty of drinks there and then it was bedtime, and then I had to be off in the morning.

My final posting with the RASC was with 165 Company to Heacham, a small village on the North Norfolk coast. The journey from Bury St Edmunds was cross country and quite difficult and when I arrived there I could find no sign of the unit. I enquired of the villagers and was told a Company had left a few days earlier and no one knew where they had gone. I phoned Bury and they had no idea either and they suggested I awaited further instructions. Having her phone number I took this opportunity to visit Budgie at Henstead. Her telephone was in a cupboard in the Billiard Room, which has now been turned into my office and which, as it caught the sun, she only visited for breakfast, and it could only be heard if she or cook were actually in the room. So I could have had a long and unplanned leave. Indeed I could have gone AWOL and no one would have been the wiser. Anyway the Army eventually found 165 Company and when I did join up with them I was not expected.

I ended up in Seaton Sluice, a town on the coast just south of Newcastle, perhaps a nice place for tourists in the summer but in winter most inhospitable. We were stationed by the shore and ate on the beach. All the food contained sand and the wind howled. I was not expected and when I did arrive they did not know what to do with me. Eventually I was given the task of making breeze blocks at which I became an expert, but this enterprise, because nothing became of my products, was not fulfilling. A Captain John Hobbs came and inspected my work and I pointed out its uselessness, but he took no action. The Captain was a Public School man and he came to a sad ending. In the fifties I was contemplating a 165 Company reunion and contacted his firm, The Imperial Typewriter Co but was informed that he had died in a crash in his sports car.

In those days not many people had driving experience or a licence and the Army decided I should take charge of a large coal lorry. When collecting a load from a mine I took a shower and the shower rooms were full of Bevin Boys, lads, mostly from the North who had opted to become miners rather than join the forces.

My next move was to Shenfield in Essex, just outside Brentwood; we were stationed in huts in the village of Hutton. There was a pub in Shenfield called The Eagle and Child, which we nicknamed The Bird and Baby. One evening I was in there when the barman said an elderly gentleman had asked after me, as I was a relative of his. He was Mr Carr who lived alone in a cottage with a large well-tendered garden with a stream running through it. He had built a number of bridges over the stream and named them after London bridges, Tower, Westminster etc. He was quite charming and on a number of occasions I was invited to tea. The connection was that his daughter, Audrey, an eccentric, red-haired woman, was married to my paternal Uncle Howard; an uncle I never liked. Audrey was a collateral descendant of Mary Shelley, the author of Frankenstein, and she had inherited some of her waywardness. Mr Carr was separated from his wife, and had not seen his daughter for many years; such behaviour ran in the family because Howard and Audrey disinherited their children, Jack and Jill. After the war, just after I had visited him, Howard wrote to Budgie saying, 'We have just been through the agonies of war and now Douglas has turned up'. No wonder he was not my favourite uncle. Incidentally a story I was told from an early age: Before the first world war, Howard, my fathers brother was arrested for being drunk in charge of a car. Howard was locked in a police cell. My grandfather rushed there and demanded the release of his son. So, in the next edition of 'Punch' there was a picture with a caption, which merely said, "We congratulate Mr Howard

Farmiloe on being educated at Harrow and Cambridge".

I got on well with Audrey, Howard's wife. Her grandson, James, when twenty-one, phoned her and offered to visit and to try and heal the family rift. She told me that he sounded such a nice young chap but still she would not see him. Audrey came to Budgie's funeral wearing trousers and she missed the Church service. She felt she was the model for Irene in Galsworthy's The Forsyte Saga and indeed Galsworthy lived next door to my cousin Nina in The Vale of Heath in Hampstead. There was speculation that he might have based his work on our family but in fact this was not correct but the Farmiloe's were a family very much in the Forsyte mould.

At Shenfield I became friendly with the administration staff and asked to be appointed to them but there were no vacancies, which was unfortunate, as I could have exercised my brain power. I recall privates Gower and Blackmore, and Corporal Rixon. Rixon was a good friend, a little older than us at 39. He was disgruntled as he felt he should have had a commission; he had worked in a bank and had been superior to various bank managers who had been commissioned. One night in The Bird and Baby we got him drunk, there was a lady, Ivy Wilson, who regularly drank there, who was very masculine and smoked a pipe. We encouraged him to date her which he did causing much merriment. But I do not want to poke fun at Ivy who was a very nice person. I kept up with her and she ran a greengrocer's shop with her sister and I was her accountant for a number of years. I got to know the CO well in Shenfield, a Major Arbuckle. He was a burly chap in his late fifties, not unlike Colonel Blimp. He had come across my family and would have liked to give me a commission if possible, but this was not possible but he did promote me to an unpaid acting lance corporal, the highest rank I achieved in the army. We were all issued with 'housewives', those little sewing kits, but in trying to sew on my new stripe I was all fingers and thumbs, so the Platoon Sergeant helped me out.

There was an important cricket match arranged against the neighbouring company and, thanks to the direct railway line to Beccles, I fetched all my cricket gear from Henstead, including my many-striped Uppingham Blazer, a garment I still have to this day and which almost fits. The match was played on the Brentwood School ground and we won with me making a few runs. However the celebrations in The Bird and Baby got out of hand and I got tipsy, roustering right up to closing time. But we had to be back by 10pm and on my return the Sergeant Major put me on a charge and, straight away, marched me to the Major's office. I was still wearing my cricket clothes including the multi-coloured blazer and I had Otto, my dachshund under my arm. Major Arbuckle was most magnanimous and congratulated me on my innings and dismissed the charge – a lucky escape. Unfortunately the Major moved on and on his departure I lost my stripe. Captain Hobbs remained and there was also Captain Tanner, a nice man, who had been a Ship's Purser. One Officer I disliked was Lieutenant Wheeler; he was full of himself and owned a Chemist's shop in Mill Hill. I decided to visit the shop after the War and get square with him, but never got around to.

There was another local besides The Bird and Baby, which was in Hutton and this was The Chequers. The Landlord was Arthur Chase who had been a purser on the P&O Lines. He was about thirty-five and for the next thirty years was a good friend of mine and, at various establishments, I was his accountant. His wife, an Officer in the Wrens, was away on duty. Friends of the Chases were the Spurrs; Captain Spurr had been a Captain on the P&O Line and held the world record for towing a distressed ship, which was 2,300 miles. They had three children, Wendy, a precocious girl of about fifteen, who always joined up with her parents in the pub and who caught the eye of many an Officer. Ironically, when she had her own children she was much stricter. Russell, the older son, was quite senior in the Navy and invariably away at sea and Michael, the younger one, was a Sub Lieutenant and often on leave. The final member of the family was a Corgi who was a regular at the pub and, when I had to move from Shenfield and not able to take Otto with me the Spurr's looked after him. The two dogs became great friends and, when I remarried, Otto and I were reunited after the War. One day a letter came from Pat saying she had some important news and in May 1944 she arrived at Hutton with Otto, having left Susan and Jay in the Isle of Wight. We met in the large reception hall and I was shattered to hear that, as she wished to marry a GI, she wanted a divorce. Without avail I pleaded with her to change her mind and then it was agreed that, with Michael staying with the Booths, I would have care of Susan and Otto. My mother took care of Susan in the meantime, and then the Spurr's offered to look after her as well as Otto she spent almost seven happy years with them. They adored her and the whole family treated her as one of their own and I could see her whenever I wanted.

Shenfield proved a good place for finding new clients for my accountancy practice; as well as Ivy Wilson and Arthur Chase I added a couple of hairdressers a local one and Mr and Mrs Furlong from Gidea Park. Later there was Jack Diamond, who I was to meet up with in St Albans, he was about thirty and a rough, amusing cockney. We joined up again after the war when he had started up as a builder. His neighbour and another builder, Mr Fox also became a client.

I was at my next posting, St Albans, for six months. My spirits were low, partly because I had no work satisfaction and the divorce was very upsetting. Pat still wrote me long daily letters about her progress and how she was preparing for the baby, which was another man's, and I knew the GI, Richard, was in the background. I was so down in the dumps that I saw the camp doctor who referred me to a psychiatrist. He recommended returning to the pay corps. The army sat on this suggestion for a while, but after some agitation they posted me to a unit in Bury, Lancashire.

I went berserk when Pat gave birth to John Raftery, her baby. I heard the news from a letter and these letters were most confusing, as she would write as though we were still a married couple. Indeed when she moved to America her letters, although only containing news of the children, caused great friction between Dorothy, my new wife, and I. When the baby was born I was granted leave and, fortunately, when we met up at the US army camp in Warrington my anger had subsided. I met Richard Raftery and he was charming and well mannered and, indeed, he was to suffer great distress when Pat left him for her next husband. I asked to see the Commanding Officer who was polite and sympathetic but he could not take any action. He remarked that it was a great worry to him that so many of his GIs were running off with British soldier's wives; 'Over here, Over Paid, Over Sexed' was the expression of the time. Then I went to the Nursing Home and demanded to see my wife. The matron suspected something was up but when I saw Pat and the baby my heart melted.

Despite everything life at St Albans was tolerable and the unit a small friendly one. 164 Company was a Service Unit and we were issued with red berets and became airborne, but as we were destined for gliders we had no air training, the plan being to land as passengers. Arnheim was approaching and everyone wearing a red beret was a potential hero. Such was the goodwill towards us that on a day's leave in the West End the Empire Cinema in Leicester Square gave me a free ticket and the meal around the corner was free as well. Had Arnheim worked the history of the Normandy Landings would have been different and many lives would have been saved. But the battle was a disaster as the Germans were ready for us. I was in the rear party located in woods behind St Albans and never called upon to go on a glider.

My first night on being posted to Bury was terrible. I found lodgings in Radcliffe and the landlady told me I had to share a double bed. My bedmate was an old man and he got fruity so I spent the remains of the night on a sofa in the sitting room. Then I found excellent lodgings with Mrs Heap and her daughter Elsie. Mrs Heap was tiny, wiry and always laughing and with a heart of gold. She treated me like a son and Elsie, who was engaged to a soldier, treated me like a brother and they were kind enough to tolerate me coming home tipsy. I was sorry to leave the Heaps but nine months later I was posted back to London. I kept in touch with them; Elsie married her soldier and she wrote to say her mother was lonely. I then had the daft idea that she should come and live and work at Henstead for my grandmother. It did not work. She was like a fish out of water and within two months she was back home. Lancashire people were amazingly friendly and kind and without airs and graces and I was sorry to leave. I have memories of catching flu and spending three days in Bury hospital. There was one brief flirtation. I dated a female Sergeant Major. She was attractive and intelligent but romance never blossomed.

One of my great army friends was Private Jock Handy. He was about thirty-five and from Kirkcaldy in Scotland and had a girl in every town. Jock had been in the Black Watch but now had a wooden leg and so was transferred to the Pay Corps. We became great buddies, he claimed he had few male companions and I was an exception and we went out drinking most evenings. He was a remarkable drinker and, being Scottish, liked chasers. His accent was broad Scots and I could just understand it. He had a girlfriend in Bury called Doris who was married. One night, when in bed with Doris, her soldier husband unexpectedly came back from leave. She hid the wooden leg under the bed and somehow Jock escaped out of the window back to his digs. I was detailed to call round next morning to collect the leg, and the husband was none the wiser. Jock came to visit me when I was posted to London and we would go out on the town. After I had married Dorothy he turned up drunk at our flat in Camden Road at 2 o'clock in the morning and slept on the stairs. Dorothy just left him there. Because of his drinking she took a dislike to him but when we were living in Chadwell Heath he came to stay. Dorothy's younger sister Laura was staying who had been living in Liverpool with a fellow called Harry. Jock charmed Laura and, much to Dorothy's disgust, a romance bloomed. In the end Dorothy kicked him out and Laura returned to Liverpool and married Harry.

I had one other notable romance towards the end of the War. Her husband was serving in the forces and she had a young son. Anyhow we fell in love but we always knew right from the start that our relationship could never go any further once her husband returned from the war. Although we knew this, it did not stop us from falling in love, and I missed her terribly when, after the war her husband returned. Some fifty years later with the help of a telephone directory I tracked her down.

I was demobbed on 16th April 1946. I remember collecting my demob suit, together with a trilby hat, shirt, socks, underwear and a pair of shoes. One had a choice of colours and mine was brown, just wearable but not Savile Row. Those recently demobbed stood out in a crowd; fortunately I had two good Savile Row suits at Henstead, which I found useful.

My first task was to find accommodation and I applied to Hampstead Borough Council stating I had the care of two children, and they offered me a very spacious and newly decorated flat in Well Walk. I discussed my good luck with fellow members of the Tunnel Club and one of them, Mrs Coleman, offered to come and be housekeeper. I had no furniture but she was moving house and brought hers. She had a strapping seventeen-year-old son who attended University College School, the Public School adjacent to my grandparent's old house. This lad was quite an athlete and was training to swim the channel. Mrs Coleman knew I had two children and that my plan was for her to look after them while I was working. I had decided that Susan should stay where she was with the Spurr's as she was doing so well there, but Michael was different. My mother wanted him in London and it was expensive keeping him at the Booth's. But then Mrs Coleman said she would not help and things got so difficult that I moved into digs, leaving the excellent flat to her. Chambers, my grandmother's old chauffeur, had married for the second time the parlour maid, Madge and they lived in the village of Carlton Colville, just a few miles from Henstead. Michael went to live with them and was very happy there and much loved by both of them. I would see him when visiting Budgie and he must have stayed there nearly a year.

I had three good friends about this time whom I had met just before leaving the Pay Corps. Alan Loseby lived in Reading at 44 Waylen Road. John Hughman was thin and tall, about 6ft 4; his father was Secretary of the National Liberal Club and he was very keen on greyhound racing where he would bet heavily. My third friend was Evans, a Major in the army and I forget his Christian name. He and I decided to visit every West End theatre, a tall order as there were about thirty, but we achieved our target. Four performances particularly stand out, Gwen Francon-Davies starring in Richard of Bordeaux, The Winslow Boy by Terence Rattigan and Young Woodley with Frank Lawton playing a schoolboy who fell in love with his Housemaster's wife. Also Wendy Hillier was good in Pygmalion.

One evening Evans told me about a car accident he had had that morning. He hit a pedestrian who was not badly hurt and a crowd gathered. They were very hostile as Evans had a posh accent. In 1946 it felt as though Britain was ripe for a social revolution. The year before when I was thirty-one and had never up until then voted, I remember seeing Winston Churchill electioneering in Mornington Crescent, Camden. The crowd was so hostile that if he had not been surrounded by bodyguards he would have been lynched. The thinking of the whole country was anti-establishment and Labour were swept to power in the following election. I was shocked by the way Churchill was treated, but after six years of war it was understandable.

On leaving the army I obtained a job with a firm of Accountants, Friend-James, Sinclair and Yarnell on Kingsway. There was two years remission for war service on my accountancy articles and I had already done two and a half so I had only another six months to do and pass the exams. Also now I was paid and with Budgie's allowance my income was adequate, but I shortly set up my own practice and so never fully qualified.

Romance was to blossom again, this time with a sweet girl, Diane, in the ATS. She was only eighteen when we met and I was thirty and she was the foster daughter of the Booth family who were looking after Michael. We saw each other over fifteen months after the end of the War. We talked of marriage and opened a joint Post Office account. She would have been a good step-mother to Michael and Susan but she was very placid and I prefer the fiery, passionate type. She wrote me over two hundred letters and I wrote back at least a hundred and fifty. Letter writing was the thing in those days; anyway Dorothy had a field day and burnt them all. I hope Diane found a good husband in the end. I felt I had let her down.

Richard Raftery had been back in America for three months, and Pat was waiting for a berth on a ship so that she could follow. She phoned me and asked to meet me at the Tunnel Club where she told me she had an embarkation date and she asked me to see her off. We were not in the club long, but by the door, the same one by which we met eight years earlier, I asked her for her new address. She hesitated and said she had better not give it to me. Did she think I would turn up and make a fuss? Should I have tried to persuade her to stay? I shall never know the answers to these questions.

I saw Pat off at the station and she had the new baby, John and Jay with her. Jay, then five, had a toy gun and was pretending to be Dick Barton, the special agent. He thought I was his father as he never knew his real one. Later when I met up with him again in America we got on well and recently stayed with him whilst in America. I kissed Pat good bye for the last time. The parting totally shattered me. It was as though my life had ended and back at my digs that night, hoping she might come home one day, I cried myself to sleep. But I soon recovered and a week or two later I met Dorothy. She reckoned that if ever Pat came back to England I would go back to her. This certainly was not the case, but Dorothy never believed me.

Pat died of cancer aged 59 in 1978. Dorothy and I were having tea one Sunday when Michael phoned. I was in shock but could not mention it to Dorothy, as she would not have sympathised. Sadly there was no one else there to talk to.

My digs were 63 Harberton Road, Archway. The landladies were three sisters from Wales; Gwen was about forty and very homely and caring and one of her younger sisters was engaged to someone in the forces. There were five lodgers and I had to share a room. In the next room was a recently demobbed soldier, John who shared with an Irishman. Paddy, who had not been in the war and worked as a salesman for Moss Bros. We got on well and every Saturday night we would go out for serious drinking sessions. On Sunday Paddy would go to confession to ask forgiveness for all his excesses. One night John, Paddy and I were in the Lyons Corner House in Regent Street, in fact the one from which Aliki, her friends and myself were thrown out of for making too much noise ten years earlier. I spied two girls sitting at a table and John volunteered to make their acquaintance. That is how I met Dorothy, my second wife. We were married thirty days later and I became a reformed character; no more chasing after women or wild drinking sessions, although I was by no means teetotal. I was now thirty-two and had to earn a living. We were married for fifty-four years and I never strayed.

CHAPTER ELEVEN

Henstead Hall

My grandfather purchased the Henstead estate in 1920 from the Barker family, who had had some connection with the church. The estate consisted of eight farms, all occupied by tenant farmers. There was about 1,600 acres in all and it stretched from the A12 to the boarders of the villages of Hulver and Wrentham. Grandfather did not acquire the living of Henstead Church, which remained with the Barkers.

The Palgrave family were relatives of the Barkers and Sir Robert Palgrave lived at the Hall and he had a lift installed which still works. The estate, together with the neighbouring Sotterley estate was run by Mr Charters who lived in the Old Rectory in Hulver. I can remember playing tennis there in the early thirties. The other diversion at that time were the Saturday night hops at the local pub, The Hulver Hut, where a good dance could be had with a local girl. My father has a memorial in Henstead Church and my first recollections of the village were in 1924 when I was nine. We would usually travel down to Southwold by train, and I would be accompanied by nurse Robinson. We changed at Halesworth and then caught the famous Southwold branch line, stopping at Wenhaston, Blythborough and Walberswick. It was said the trains went up hills so slowly that passengers could get out, pick flowers, and then rejoin at the top; I sadly cannot remember doing this myself. As I mentioned earlier when I first came down to this part of the world I spent my time at grandfather's other house in Field Style Road, Southwold. Between this house and the Church was a green, to be found just over a style where, much to my grandfather's disgust I played cricket with the local boys. When short of funds we had a cunning, and always successful, plan. Leading onto the common was a gate, which was kept open during the day for cars, but shut at night. We would shut the gate and demand a penny from each driver to open it. Near the gate was the local cinema, sadly now closed, and not to be confused with another one of the same name in Blackmill Road. These 'highway man' funds paid for the cinema entrance; Lillian Gish and Ronald Colman were our staple fare.

My other great interest was the local Postman, Mr Brown, then about twenty-five years old. I would get up at six in the morning and meet him leaving the Post Office in the High Street and help him deliver letters; consequently

I knew every street and house in the town. If I was a bit late I could always catch up with him. When I moved permanently down to Suffolk in 1960 Mr Brown was still alive and living in Wangford, but stupidly I did not look him up.

Although grandfather owned Henstead Hall I do not think he ever slept there; we would visit to supervise work on the estate, the two of us travelling on bicycles from Southwold. The journey was better when grandmother came as we travelled by car and there was an excellent tea at The Spread Eagle at Wrentham. The gardens at Henstead were kept in tip top condition. The lawns were mowed by a pony that wore special shoes to protect the turf. The Head gardener was a Mr Bailey, who lived in the thatched cottage in Church Road, and he had two assistants. His son, who worked with his father, and did some work for Dorothy and I in the sixties, lived in Well Lane, and then retired to Kessingland.

In front of the Hall was a large paddock and in the woods behind was a gamekeeper's cottage occupied by Mr Thrower. The bricks are still around from this cottage, which has now been demolished. The house where clients of mine, the Hunts, now live was occupied by Mrs Howlett. She worked for Dorothy in the Hall when we ran it as a hotel. The grounds contained a walled garden, which, in its hay day, was magnificent, hosting figs, peaches and pears, a veritable Eden. Also the acre of orchard just beyond with its apples, pears and plums was a paradise for a small boy to explore. Grandfather created a cricket pitch between the Church and Rushmere Road. The Hampstead cricketers came down to play and as a boy I joined in on their practice.

Prime's Garage in the village thrived between the wars and up to twenty men were employed repairing both cars and agricultural machinery; business came from all over Suffolk. Mrs Prime ran the village shop from a house next door to where Andy Bond, the village mechanic, now lives. Groceries were her mainstay but I was interested in the sweets.

When my grandfather died in 1931 my grandmother obviously did not need three houses. She sold Avening House, Hampstead and gave up Field Style Road and in 1933 made her permanent home at Henstead, the year I left school. I would make many visits but did not live there as I had all the attractions of London to occupy me. Grandmother died in 1960, one year short of her one hundredth birthday and in my early years she meant more to me than anybody else. My father was the eldest of eight children and was no doubt her favourite and, following his death in action, her love passed to me.

The family were horrified when grandmother sold the house in Hampstead and, aged 72, moved to Henstead. As years went by they tried to persuade her to move somewhere smaller but she preferred to stay where she was all alone. Henstead has a draw on people; I am following in her footsteps and have no intention of leaving. Dorothy often wanted to return to London but I refused.

Grandmother, or Budgie, as she was known to me, lived in some style up to 1939; she brought a number of servants with her from London as well as the Daimler Double Six and chauffeur and entertained quite a bit. Then, during the Second World War, the Army took over half the house, all the outbuildings and the woods. There were machine guns there and also a fellow called Denis Long from Cornwall was stationed with us. He eventually married Joyce, the daughter of Mrs Crane, the landlady of The Hulver Gate and after her death they took over the licence. Valerie, their daughter, still lives in Hulver and Denis's sister also came from Cornwall and married Billy Wright, who lived in a caravan on the Hulver Road.

After the war, in 1948, it was decided by the family that the estate should be sold. All the farms were sold to the tenants and the house, woods and some cottages sold to Watts, a timber merchant from Bungay; many of the willows from the woods became cricket bats. A condition of the sale was that Budgie could stay on as a life tenant on a peppercorn rent. She lived on in genteel poverty as the money did not go to her but into grandfather's complicated Trust and she was too old to bother about things. The house was never painted although the Farmiloes owned a paint firm and by 1960 everything was very dilapidated and not restored until Dorothy, with hard work, turned it around. The front drive was overgrown with grass and one day, a year before Budgie died, a local newspaper reporter came along as he had heard that an old lady was living in a derelict house. Of course both relatives and I visited. In 1955 the central heating boiler blew up and was never replaced. Instead of lighting a fire she would sit in the living room in the depth of winter covered in paper to keep warm, but when I visited she did, in fact light a fire. The only help she had was Herbert, the Gardener, who lived in a thatched cottage on the estate and in 1955 there was a fatal accident when a builder climbing a ladder to repair a gutter by the back door fell and killed himself.

Occasionally Budgie went to London to visit relatives and she was also keen on films and was known in her nineties to walk all the way to Lowestoft Road about four miles to catch a bus to Norwich. Also she went to the Cinema in Lowestoft and sat in the front row with the kids so as to get the best view.

When she first arrived in Henstead she intended to carry on with her charity work, but village people are funny and they viewed newcomers with suspicion. Budgie was snubbed and never tried again. Just before she died she confided in me that at last she felt she had been accepted. I was glad that this was so as I intended to adopt a career in local politics.

Today, however, the make-up of the village is totally different. Budgie did allow the local fete to be held at Henstead and Dorothy kept the tradition going. Only the other day Mrs Raven of the village told me that as a small girl she had to present a bouquet to Budgie and spent much time practising her curtsey. One of Budgie's daughters, Winifred, lived there when not away on holiday but generally the only person there was the cook, Mrs Pullen. She had connections with us for many years and I remember in 1923, aged seven, when I fell of my tricycle and damaged my knee she looked after me while my grandparents were in the South of France. Mrs Pullen's relations lived in Canada and she would have liked to join them but she would never abandon Budgie. When Mrs Pullen was 85 and Budgie 95 it was Budgie who put Mrs Pullen in a Nursing Home in Beccles. Mrs Higgins was the cook for the final years. Her son had a bicycle shop in Kessingland and she moved into a cottage in Toad Road and ran a shop there after Budgie died. Later a Mr Lizari lived there. During the war I would come down on leave and was met at Beccles Station by Mr Sawyer, the owner of the garage at Wrentham. His taxi was challenged when going over the nearby aerodrome to collect me and Henstead Hall was surrounded by barbed wire. When this was done Budgie complained to the Officer in charge saying she could not get in or out so they cut out a section for her to get through. The men slept in the stables and up until 1960 you could see some of their graffiti involving Nazi motifs. The Army HQ was in the house and also the Officers slept there, which was company for Budgie. I have wartime letters from her describing the conditions, as indeed I have the letters from 1907 to 1917 between my grandmother and father telling stories from that war. The house had long shutters which were used for the blackout and which she closed every evening. In 1959 I had a call from aunt Winifred to say that my grandmother was seriously ill after falling off a ladder trying to close the shutters. I recall looking at the skies when taking the dog out for a walk that evening exactly as I had done 27 years earlier when leaving Uppingham. I went down the next day and was able to see her before she passed away. She hated being looked after by a nurse, as she told me, this was typical of Budgie. She died in January 1960.

I came to Henstead in August 1960 and there was much dereliction and neglect. When the Army left Budgie decided she was too old to modernise things, anyway she did not have the money. I had little money but Dorothy, my wife was a workaholic and set too. Firstly we re-established the driveway then, one by one, each room was restored. Dorothy did most of the work as I was often in London attending to my accountancy practice.

After about two years I became involved in village affairs. We formed a committee entitled The Friends of Henstead and Hulver and I have a picture of a meeting in my front room taken about 1963 of the members. There is Dorothy, myself, Owen and Joan Talbot, Shirley, my daughter, Beryl Friend and the Revd McIntyre. Our principal aim was fundraising and we had a number of over-sixties and children's parties. The over sixties are sadly no longer with us and the children all grown up. I continued Budgie's tradition and held the annual fete at the Hall, which added to the funds, and there were Bingo evenings in The Hulver Hut and Henstead School where I was an adept caller......'Legs Eleven', 'Two Fat Ladies', and 'Sweet Sixteen' were my watchwords. A big venture was the Barn Dance held just outside Henstead; word of this event spread around and we sold over two thousand tickets, a band was hired, a raffle held, with Owen Talbot drawing the tickets and me reading the numbers out. There was a good first prize, which was won by Dorothy so we had a quick redraw. I was not very popular with Dorothy after that.

We were lucky in having excellent Clergymen in the village. The Revd Cotton was the Vicar at Wrentham and later served at Sandringham and in Canada, and the Revd McIntyre was the Curate at Henstead. Both had been builders before taking the cloth and were in their mid-forties. The Revd Cotton would go straight from Church, disrobe and to The Five Bells for a pint. The Revd McIntire was married and his main concern was Henstead were he organised excellent children's outings. He blotted his copybook when he fell for a young lass, escaping defrocking, he returned to Ipswich and after a period of penance returned to the fold, but died sometime later.

Looking back I have had a roller coaster of a life. I must ask the question, 'Do I regret spending all my inheritance on women, drink and a life of luxury? The answer – you bet I don't. Have I learnt any lessons over the years? The answer – none'. The words 'Retirement' and 'Savings' are not in my vocabulary. I am always overdrawn. On holiday I enjoy the best hotels, and live in a big house, albeit only half of it, and I drive a Rolls. Over the years I have been lucky enough to receive windfalls – three Farmiloe legacies and the sale of my London Practice. What did I do? – Pay off my debts and start spending. I enjoy living from day to day. It keeps me going and I shall do so until I reach one hundred. I always give this advice to my clients, 'Do as I say, not what I do.'

A Word on Alaric (Born 1900)

He was educated at Harrow and Cambridge and as will be seen on the photo a very dapper individual. He had a breakdown in the latter twenties and was never heard to speak again. The war completely passed him by.

I recall my grandparents discussing the problems when we were all on holiday in Southwold during the late twenties. In consequence Henstead Hall was opened for him and Fred Corkerey was appointed his nurse. Whenever he went on his bike he had to be followed at a reasonable distance by Corkerey. When he left there was a succession of other nurses who did not stay long. His experience as a cyclist soon lost them as he would go at full speed up and down a hill to lose them. On one occasion he even cycled to Newmarket to place a bet, which was 60 miles away.

He would spend his time in his sitting room and had his own bathroom and bedroom. Waited on every day and was allowed two bottles of beer a day and smoked incessantly.

It must have been a source of worry for my grandmother for the last twenty years of her life as no nurses were available. On one occasion he had gone up to bed but previously had fallen asleep and set light to the sofa. The result was Budgie and Mrs Pullen both in their eighties had to lift the sofa out of the window and onto the flower bed outside to avoid a bad fire.

Besides smoking his cigarettes he would study the race cards and we found out later that he had made notes of all the times of the trains.

It was a worry to Budgie as the Police on occasion escorted him home. He was a familiar face to the local lads who teased him. He exposed himself to those passing and was obviously a paedophile whom in these days would be registered as a Sex Offender. If visitors came they would call in and say hello and he would smile whether he knew them at all but obviously never spoke.

From 1960-63 after my grandmother's death we looked after him until his decease.

I recall one day when it was particularly cold Dorothy made a fire up in the sitting room. As soon as he returned from his cycle ride he just stamped on the fire and put it out.

THE SPOON RE-POLISHED

By Mid 1947 I was completing my Articles with a firm of Chartered Accountants at £6 per week salary and an allowance from my grandmother. So life was bearable.

<u>Work</u>

By July 1947 I had a wife with a daughter of five years old to provide for. Soon after my marriage to my new wife, to her credit persuaded me to give up taking the allowance from my grandmother. Until this moment I had never worked hard having always one eye on the clock.

Now I had to, so I started up my own Accountancy Practice in 1948 and which I'm still working hard at in 2010.

To begin with I used to do Sub Contracting from other Accountants and received 40% of the fee. Hard work but it produced cash to live on. During this time I went looking for private clients. How easy it was in the late 1940's. So many coming out of the Services wanted to start up in business on their own. It was all so easy you could pick one client up in a street and then in a very short time you found you had half a dozen clients. Clusters of clients, except strangely I have never had a client from my hometown of Hampstead.

It soon got to the stage where I had too many clients. Answer was to take on a partner. This happened on four occasions but I was always the Senior Partner. This resulted in a considerable cash benefit to me and there was no Capital Gains about until 1965.

I was not made for partnerships so in every case I left the partnership to be on my own.

The breaking up was always at my request but always amicably arranged. I suppose I am a character who likes to be in full control without consulting anyone else.

In those days Limited Companies were popular to clients in business. There were not the complications and restrictions of today. During the years successive Governments have brought in rules relating to those qualified to act as Auditors. Every hurdle as an unqualified Accountant I was fortunate to overcome. My experience rather than any qualification always pulled me through. Today many of my clients are Limited Companies and not being a Chartered Accountant has never hindered my work. However it is one of my personal regrets in life that I cannot put Chartered Accountant after my name. However I joined the Association of Authorised Public Accountants which was formed for experienced accountants who had not sat any examinations. Very fortunately for me this association was accepted by the board of trade to qualify as auditors along with chartered and certified accountants. In return I do have to complete 40 hours of Continued Professional Development.

When I moved to Suffolk in 1960 I had to sell 50% of my clients in London and did not have a local client. Gradually I established a local practice, which even today brings in new clients. I still have a few London clients left and I have some in the South of England.

Have always had excellent staff and this I have been most fortunate. Today I couldn't wish for two more excellent ladies who work for me. (One has been with me for over 20 years). They are more than capable of running the practice as I do spend less time there these days.

My office is completely up to date and needs to be as so much is done online these days. But I have a confession; I have never been on a computer and never will. My two excellent ladies are more than competent to sort this out.

RESPECTABILITY

The Silver Spoon was definitely Re-Polished from the 1970's onwards.
To the outside world I was a most respectable Gentleman. I lived in a mansion with thirty rooms and 15 Acres of Land. I ran my own Accountancy Practice and I was both a County and District Councillor having served on each for 15 years. I was Chairman of the Parish Council for a number of years and a Governor of two schools. I allowed the Annual Village Fete to be held at Henstead Hall, which followed my grandmother's tradition. I held dinners here for the over sixties and the children of the Village. In 1980 I gave up my beloved Jaguars for Rolls Royces.

What more could be expected to dispel my carefree youth and of course, my marriage was stable, which in fact lasted 54 years.

Money

Money and I parted company prior to the War with alacrity. One would have thought that I had learnt my lesson but no! Even to this very day I need to spend. I never know from week to week how much will be available to live on. It is I suppose an excitement having never lived on a fixed salary. As Mr Micawber said: Annual income £20, annual expenditure £19.19/6, result happiness. Annual income £20. annual expenditure £20.0/6, result misery. I never took Micawber's advice and something always turns up.

I had a decent enough income to live on with my practice and my wife running the Hotel, but it was not enough for extras. We still managed to take holidays in England and the Channel Islands and stay at the best hotels. From 1980 we went on the Continent twice a year plus an annual separate visit to Paris (19 years in a row). From 1990 visits across the Atlantic has occurred on 21 occasions.

How did it all happen and as well as breaks spent monies on cars, fur coats & luxuries. Well something always turned up just in time as for example sale of my clients, small Inheritance, sale of woodland and conversion of stables to houses, to sell. There was always something. Really no difference in 2010 as it was in 1936.

I do not think that my later success would have been possible without my second wife, Dorothy as she was a workaholic and a perfectionist. When we moved to Henstead Hall she decorated every one of the thirty rooms, which except for the very tall rooms in the house including the ceilings. She was adept at wallpapering. I was only allowed to do the painting of the outside, a task, which I really enjoyed on two occasions. I didn't mind heights but usually got covered with paint. Dorothy had never cooked for numbers but finished up with catering for 45 persons. On the two occasions she employed Chefs and these turned out to be in her eyes unsatisfactory. In consequence their employment was only a short one.

Dorothy was also a very keen gardener and spent many hours on this pastime. In addition she was crazy about animals and birds and at one stage had over 150 pets. In addition she ran a Cattery, and I boarded up to 12 dogs in Kennels.

This marriage, which lasted 54 years sounds perfect. We were both faithful to each other during this time. However now for the downside, she was without doubt the most jealous woman one could encounter and the scenes created both sides of the Atlantic Ocean would make a most interesting book of short stories. Some of the scenes she displayed were beyond belief. I learnt to be placid, take the brunt but at the same time being very obstinate I survived these attacks. One in a marriage is supposed to give and take but every decision of what we did, where we went to on holiday and how the money was to be spent I had the final word. I may have lost every battle but I won the war. No one could have survived the encounters without the result of eventually winning.

The last four years of Dorothy's life when dementia crept in completely changed her character. She became extremely loveable to others and myself at this stage.

Of course there were times when we got on well but the outcome of all this was I had two families. We had no children together but I was able to bring up three generations who unusually all call me dad. I am extremely fortunate in old age that I have a son and daughter in the States plus grandchildren and very many great grandchildren whom I see often. Back in this country I am looked after by Dorothy's granddaughter and great granddaughter, who look upon me as their Dad and I in turn look upon them as my Daughters. (Dorothy's Daughter died the year after Dorothy). To top all this when I sold the front half of Henstead Hall to strangers I was accepted as one of their family.

What is the secret of Old Age? To my mind it is always look forward and to have many interests as is possible. I still run my accountancy practice and still aim for targets. I still drive, smoke a pipe but do not consume as much liquor as before. I have had my share in my lifetime.
Hobbies are essential I enjoy soaps and reality shows as relaxation and also read a lot. This is confined to the opposite taste of TV and relates to history of most periods, which I do have good knowledge.

Another hobby is the organisation of Reunions and during my lifetime have clocked up over 60, which covers Ex County Councillors, Family and School. I still get passionate about the Arsenal and Uppingham. All these activities keep me going but to write further memoirs is a task I will not undertake again. It has been a mammoth undertaking but am pleased to have the satisfaction.

I think on the whole my life can be summed up in the familiar words of Frank Sinatra 'I DID IT MY WAY'